D1457107

5⁰⁰
80K

WORLD BANK STAFF WORKING PAPERS
Number 578

MANAGEMENT AND DEVELOPMENT SERIES
Number 5

Development Finance Companies, State and Privately Owned

A Review

David L. Gordon

The World Bank
Washington, D.C., U.S.A.

HG
3726
.G65
1983

Copyright © 1983
The International Bank for Reconstruction
and Development / THE WORLD BANK
1818 H Street, N.W.
Washington, D.C. 20433, U.S.A.

All rights reserved
Manufactured in the United States of America
First printing July 1983
Second printing January 1985

This is a working document published informally by the World Bank. To present the results of research with the least possible delay, the typescript has not been prepared in accordance with the procedures appropriate to formal printed texts, and the World Bank accepts no responsibility for errors. The publication is supplied at a token charge to defray part of the cost of manufacture and distribution.

The World Bank does not accept responsibility for the views expressed herein, which are those of the authors and should not be attributed to the World Bank or to its affiliated organizations. The findings, interpretations, and conclusions are the results of research supported by the Bank; they do not necessarily represent official policy of the Bank. The designations employed, the presentation of material, and any maps used in this document are solely for the convenience of the reader and do not imply the expression of any opinion whatsoever on the part of the World Bank or its affiliates concerning the legal status of any country, territory, city, area, or of its authorities, or concerning the delimitation of its boundaries, or national affiliation.

The full range of World Bank publications, both free and for sale, is described in the *Catalog of Publications;* the continuing research program is outlined in *Abstracts of Current Studies.* Both booklets are updated annually; the most recent edition of each is available without charge from the Publications Sales Unit, Department T, The World Bank, 1818 H Street, N.W., Washington, D.C. 20433, U.S.A., or from the European Office of the Bank, 66 avenue d'Iéna, 75116 Paris, France.

David L. Gordon prepared this paper as a consultant to the World Development Report core team.

Library of Congress Cataloging in Publication Data

Gordon, David L. (David Livingston), 1916-
    Development finance companies, state and privately
owned.

    (World Bank staff working papers ; no. 578)
    Includes bibliographical references.
    1. Development credit corporations. 2. Development
banks. I. Title. II. Series.
HG3726.G65   1983   332.2   83-12552
ISBN 0-8213-0226-4

Abstract

Development finance companies (DFCs) are designed, and have been set up, in virtually all developing countries, mainly to provide term financing for industrial investment--a need that was largely neglected by commercial banks in those countries prior to the 1960s. The DFCs were also expected to promote, in various ways, growth and diversification of the financial sector. Many early DFCs, notably those fostered by the World Bank, were privately owned, although with encouragement and often financial subsidy from government. Increasingly over the years, state ownership has become more common.

While differences among DFCs--in institutional structure, management style, financial performance, and other attributes--are apparently due more to differing country circumstances or clienteles than to their ownership, certain tendencies are somewhat more frequent or strongly evident in state-owned than in private DFCs, and vice versa. These are examined, with illustrative examples.

The difficulties of resource mobilization that particularly face private DFCs are discussed as well as the strategies being used by some to meet this problem, including entry into money market and commercial financing and linkages with commercial banks. Meanwhile, some of the latter are moving more into term lending, further obscuring the demarcation between them and DFCs. Recognizing that in most developing countries the key role in industrial financing is likely to fall on government-owned DFCs, suggestions are made as to possible means of mitigating the problem of undue political influence in their operations.

Acknowledgments

Comments and suggestions by World Bank staff on an earlier draft are gratefully acknowledged. J. Chanmugan was especially helpful in refreshing and correcting my memory of details and in clarifying certain concepts, and Mary Shirley in suggesting a number of points for further discussion. However, responsibility for both the substance and presentation of this paper is entirely mine.

Papers in the Management and Development Series

1. Agarwala, Ramgopal. <u>Price Distortions and Growth in Developing Countries</u>. World Bank Staff Working Paper no. 575.

2. Agarwala, Ramgopal. <u>Planning in Developing Countries: Lessons of Experience</u>. World Bank Staff Working Paper no. 576.

3. Cochrane, Glynn. <u>Policies for Strengthening Local Government in Developing Countries</u>. World Bank Staff Working Paper no. 582.

4. Gordon, David. <u>Development Finance Companies, State and Privately Owned: A Review</u>. World Bank Staff Working Paper no. 578.

5. Gould, David J., and Jose A. Amaro-Reyes. <u>The Effects of Corruption on Administrative Performance: Illustrations from Developing Countries</u>. World Bank Staff Working Paper no. 580.

6. Knight, Peter T. <u>Economic Reform in Socialist Countries: The Experiences of China, Hungary, Romania, and Yugoslavia</u>. World Bank Staff Working Paper no. 579.

7. Kubr, Milan, and John Wallace. <u>Successes and Failures in Meeting the Management Challenge: Strategies and Their Implementation</u>. World Bank Staff Working Paper no. 585.

8. Lethem, Francis J., and Lauren Cooper. <u>Managing Project-Related Technical Assistance: The Lessons of Success</u>. World Bank Staff Working Paper no. 586.

9. Ozgediz, Selcuk. <u>Managing the Public Service in Developing Countries: Issues and Prospects</u>. World Bank Staff Working Paper no. 583.

10. Paul, Samuel. <u>Training for Public Administration and Management in Developing Countries: A Review</u>. World Bank Staff Working Paper no. 584.

11. Rondinelli, Dennis A., John R. Nellis, and G. Shabbir Cheema. <u>Decentralization in Developing Countries: A Review of Recent Experience</u>. World Bank Staff Working Paper no. 581.

12. Shinohara, Miyohei, Toru Yanagihara, and Kwang Suk Kim. <u>The Japanese and Korean Experiences in Managing Development</u>. Ed. Ramgopal Agarwala. World Bank Staff Working Paper no. 574.

13. Shirley, Mary M. <u>Managing State-Owned Enterprises</u>. World Bank Staff Working Paper no. 577.

Foreword

This study is one in a series of World Bank Staff Working Papers devoted to issues of development management. Prepared as background papers for the World Development Report 1983, they provide an in-depth treatment of the subjects dealt with in Part II of the Report. The thirteen papers cover topics ranging from comprehensive surveys of management issues in different types of public sector institutions (for example, state-owned enterprises, the public service, and local government agencies) to broad overviews of such subjects as planning, management training, technical assistance, corruption, and decentralization.

The central concern underlying these papers is the search for greater efficiency in setting and pursuing development goals. The papers focus on the role of the state in this process, stress the importance of appropriate incentives, and assess the effectiveness of alternative institutional arrangements. They offer no general prescriptions, as the developing countries are too diverse--politically, culturally, and in economic resources-- to allow the definition of a single strategy.

The papers draw extensively on the experiences of the World Bank and other international agencies. They were reviewed by a wide range of readership from developing and developed countries inside and outside the Bank. They were edited by Victoria Macintyre. Rhoda Blade-Charest, Banjonglak Duangrat, Jaunianne Fawkes, and Carlina Jones prepared the manuscripts for publication.

I hope that these studies will be useful to practitioners and academicians of development management around the world.

Pierre Landell-Mills
Staff Director
World Development Report 1983

Contents

Acronyms

Aliadas/Colombia	–	Corporacion Financiera Aliadas
BAPINDO/Indonesia	–	Bank Pembanqunam, Indonesia
BCD/Cameroon	–	Banque Camerounaise de Développement
BDC/Botswana	–	Bostwana Development Corporation, Ltd.
BDET/Tunisia	–	Banque de Développement Économique Tunisienne
BDRN/Niger	–	Banque de Développement de la Republique du Niger
BIDI/Ivory Coast	–	Banque Ivorianne de Développement Industriel
BISA/Bolivia	–	Banco Industrial S.A.
BMDC/Mautitania	–	Banque Mauritanienne pour le Développement et le Commerce
BND/Upper Volta	–	Banque Nationale de Développement
BNDE/Brazil	–	Banco Nacional do Desenvolvimento Economico
BNDE/Morocco	–	Banque Nationale de Développement Économique
BSB/Bangladesh	–	Bangladesh Shilpa Bank
Caldas/Colombia	–	Corporacion Financiera de Caldas
CDB/Cyprus	–	Cyprus Development Bank
CDC/Taiwan	–	China Development Corporation
CFN/Ecuador	–	Corporacion Financiera Nacional
CFP/Colombia	–	Corporacion Financiera Popular
CIH/Morocco	–	Crédit Immobilier et Hotelier
CNB/Korea	–	Citizens National Bank
COFIEC/Ecuador	–	Ecuatoriana de Desarrollo S.A. – Compania Financiera
Colombiana/Colombia	–	Corporacion Financiera Colombiana
DBM/Mauritius	–	Development Bank of Mauritius
DBP/Philippines	–	Development Bank of the Philippines
DBS/Singapore	–	Development Bank of Singapore
DBZ/Zambia	–	Development Bank of Zambia
DFCC/Sri Lanka	–	Development Finance Company of Ceylon
DIB/Egypt	–	Development Industrial Bank
EMENA	–	Europe, Middle East, and North Africa
financiera	–	Collective term for the numerous finance companies (corporaciones financieras), often having a regional base, in Colombia and Ecuador.
IBS/Sudan	–	Industrial Bank of Sudan
ICC/Ireland	–	Industrial Credit Company
ICICI/India	–	Industrial Credit and Investment Company of India
IDB/Kenya	–	Industrial Development Bank
IDBI/India	–	Industrial Development Bank of India
IDBI/Israel	–	Industrial Development Bank of Israel
IDBP/Pakistan	–	Industrial Development Bank of Pakistan
IFCI/India	–	International Finance Corporation of India
IFCT/Thailand	–	International Finance Corporation of Thailand
IFF/Finland	–	Industrialization Fund of Finland
IMDBI/Iran	–	Industry and Mining Development Bank of Iran
INDEBANK/Malawi	–	Investment and Development Bank of Malawi, Ltd.
KDB/Korea	–	Korea Development Bank
KDFC-KLB/Korea	–	Korea Development Finance Corporation, which later became the Korea Long Term Credit Bank
KIE/Kenya	–	Kenya Industrial Estates
KLB	–	Korea Long Term Credit Bank (see KDFC)
LBDI/Liberia	–	Liberian Bank for Development and Investment

LIBOR	–	London Interbank Offered Rate
LNDC/Lesotho	–	Lesotho National Development Corporation
Nacional/Colombia	–	Corporacion Financiera Nacional
NIBID/Greece	–	National Investment Bank for Industrial Development
Norte/Colombia	–	Corporacion Financiera del Norte
NDFC/Pakistan	–	National Development Finance Corporation
NIB/Ghana	–	National Investment Bank
NIBID/Greece	–	National Investment Bank for Industrial Development, S.A.
NIDB/Nigeria	–	Nigerian Industrial Development Bank, Ltd.
Occidente/Colombia	–	Corporacion Financiera de Occidente
PDCP/Philippines	–	Private Development Corporation of the Philippines
PDFCI/Indonesia	–	Private Development Finance Corporation of Indonesia
PICIC/Pakistan	–	Pakistan Industrial Credit and Investment Corporation
PISO/Philippines	–	Philippine Industrial Systems Organization
Santander/Colombia	–	Corporacion Financiera de Santander
SMI	–	Small and medium industry
SMIB/Korea	–	Small and Medium Industry Bank
SOFIDE/Zaire	–	Societe Financiere de Developpement
SOFISEDIT/Senegal	–	Societe Financiere Senegalesse pour le Developpement Industriel et Touristique
SSE	–	Small-scale industry
TDFL/Tanzania	–	Tanganyika Development Finance Company, Ltd.
TIB/Tanzania	–	Tanzania Investment Bank
TSKB/Turkey	–	Turkiye Sinai Kalkinma Bankasi, S.A.
Valle/Colombia	–	Corporacion Financiera del Valle

I. Introduction

1.   Economic development in any country both depends on and contributes to growth and diversification of the financial sector. Economic growth and fluctuations are measured largely by the aggregate data emanating from financial sector transactions. The rate and character of development, meanwhile, are influenced by the priorities and efficiency of the sector's institutions and instruments. They are the means by which savings are mobilized for investments and are transferred from low-yielding to higher yielding uses; and by which savers and investors diversify risk, can anticipate reliable returns or enhanced security or liquidity, and are thus encouraged to make longer term commitments for purposes beyond their personal horizons. As well, they are the means by which fluctuations in the economy and in the resource needs of the public sector are smoothed out and short-term funding routinely supplied. In other words, these institutions and instruments are the key mechanisms for adjustment and lubrication of an increasingly large, complex, and dynamic economic system.

2.   Developed countries have evolved a variety of financial institutions to meet the special needs of different segments of financial markets: commercial and savings banks, mortgage banks, merchant and investment banks, other thrift institutions (savings and loan associations, credit unions), development finance companies (DFCs), insurance companies, stock exchanges, securities dealers and brokers, underwriters, commercial and household finance companies, mututal funds, leasing companies, and so on. They all interact, complementing and competing with each other, and are surrounded by diverse ancillary services and regulatory mechanisms.

3.   Most of this institutional array is outside the scope of the present paper, which is concerned primarily with the management style and practices of the prototype DFC, and with a comparison of government-owned and private institutions. The term development finance company is the World Bank's designation for an institutional model (earlier and elsewhere called development bank) that was to complement the conventional commercial banking system. It was expected to help create and fill in part the need for more complex financial services in a modernizing economy. The extent to which the DFC has done so and has itself adjusted to the resulting changes in the environment of the financial sector is also discussed.

II. Evolution and Function of DFCs

4.   Commercial banks have existed in virtually all countries since the nineteenth century and have gradually replaced traditional moneylenders and other informal intermediaries. The basic function of banks has been to attract and assemble household savings and to provide short-term funding for the temporary needs of traders, artisans, commercial agriculture and, over time, for more sophisticated production and commerce. But, typically, banks have been less responsive to long-term credit needs--especially those of evolving industrial sectors--because of their inadequate resource base, risk aversion, low profitability, and so on.

5.   Basically, industrial term lending runs counter to their institutional habits, attitudes, criteria, and procedures. Most commercial bank loans involve the commitment of funds for no more than a few months, and they largely finance goods in import-export trade or inventories, which themselves constitute reliable collateral. The loans usually go to firms with

an established financial record, so that a reasonable evaluation requires merely ticking off a few standard indicators of security ratios and credit rating. The financing of industrial investment, by contrast, calls for a long-term commitment, often a decade or more (and the loan is based on collateral of uncertain salability in case of default), perhaps to entrepreneurs with limited experience in the industry (often entirely new entrants). Furthermore, an industry's viability depends on numerous factors (technology, marketing, economic fluctuations, government policies, management) that can be assessed only over a span of several years, and with some expertise. This time frame and the expertise required are largely alien to traditional commercial banking.

Creation of DFCs

6.   During the first decades of international concern for development (1948-1968), the many diagnostic missions sent to asses the potential and the needs of specific developing countries almost always identified inadequate long-term credit as a central problem. Virtually all these missions recommended the creation or strengthening of a DFC as a principal means to its solution. The DFCs were to be provided with substantial long-term financial resources, which they would then allocate, in accordance with agreed policy guidelines and accepted appraisal criteria and methodology, for loans or equity investments to projects (mainly industrial) of high priority and good economic or financial return. They were commonly subsidized by a government loan at low or no interest, so subordinated as to be quasi-equity. Eventually, however, the DFCs were to mobilize resources on their own in the market. Thus, the insufficiency of long-term funding for the industrial sector and other productive purposes would be mitigated. Also, the quality of investment choices and projects would be improved through more rational

appraisals, and systematic loan follow-up would help to ensure the success of projects.

7.   In retrospect, certain questions arise: Could these ends only have been achieved by establishing and subsidizing a new class of institutions? Or, should governments and international lenders have devised systems of directives and incentives that would have induced the existing commercial banks to extend their lending horizon, undertake more aggressive term transformation, and upgrade the quality of their project appraisals and supervision? And should they have given priority to creating a policy environment that would have promoted mobilization of long-term investment funds through market forces? These questions are given added relevance by the recent widespread trend on the part of commercial banks and DFCs to combine or take on each other's functions (see paras. 33, 70, and 76-79). At first view, such alternate approaches might be expected to reduce fragmentation of the financial sector, hasten the development of genuine capital markets, make it easier for governments to influence these markets and implement development policies, and make better use of scarce managerial talent and experience. Yet, one cannot really predict by hindsight how such approaches would have worked in various countries. Consider, for example, the institutional issue.

8.   <u>Institutional Alternatives</u>. A number of governments have effectively used a combination of policy guidelines, specific directives, and financial incentives to influence the allocation and terms of commercial bank credits, among other things, to increase substantially the proportion of term loans. India and the Republic of Korea offer good examples. Both countries, however, initiated these measures after an array of DFCs had already been formed to cater to diverse clienteles, and applied them in parallel with DFC

operations. The commercial bank lending for investment needs, therefore, was not a substitute for, but a supplement to, the lending of the DFCs.

9.   In both India and Korea the large commercial banks (as well as most of the DFCs) are now state owned, but were not earlier; this is true also for many other developing countries. Indeed, through the 1950s and beyond, the commercial banking system in much of the developing world was not only under private, but also under foreign, control. This situation made it much harder to impose government policies and priorities on commercial bank lending. Such imposition would have risked a confrontation that might have had wide repercussions. Thus, cooperation had to be sought through moral suasion, negotiation, or financial incentives. Although incentives (for example, cheap advances or rediscounts from the central bank for favored loan categories) might have been persuasive, the capabilities of the monetary authorities were still quite limited--by law and resource constraints--and were taken up with other concerns. These authorities were primarily responsible for short-term stabilization and payments problems, which dictated the credit restrictions applied to the commercial banks--restrictions that were by and large irrelevant to DFC-type operations.

10.   So, rather than try to accommodate all the anomalies into existing commercial banks, at that stage (1950s, early 1960s) developing countries found it easier to create new institutions that would be clearly distinguished by function from mainstream commercial banking and that would not be saddled with the tradition and attitudes of the existing foreign-based organizations. 1/ These new institutions would be able to recruit staff and set compensation and career paths without having to fight an entrenched corporate bureaucracy, and they would be easily excludable from inappropriate monetary regulations and restrictions. When the existing commercial banks were called upon to play an

important development investment role and were successful (as was the State Bank of India), they then had to set up separate organizational units, establish quite different loan appraisal and administration criteria, and give intensive special training to the staff. In effect, they set up a DFC within the parent bank.

11.   Policy Environment. Whether the prototype DFCs might have delayed or hampered the development of more broadly based, private, long-term capital markets is difficult to judge. By providing acceptable channels for external financing (seen as the crucially scarce factor) to the private industrial sector, the DFC formula on one hand helped to defer politically unpalatable decisions as to interest rates and investment incentives; meanwhile, domestic resources continued to be mobilized and allocated largely by administrative fiat. On the other hand, governments in the aid-giving countries, notably the United States in the early development decades, were eager precisely to promote and use such channels, and were not overly concerned about the possibly adverse effects of their subsidized capital structure on the emergence of competing institutions. 2/ All political and psychological pressures weighed in favor of the accelerated application of resources, external and domestic, to industrial investment. Even if the local authorities (or indeed the aid givers) had been sure of how to stimulate market forces in the early stages of financial sector development, it is hard to imagine that the mere absence of the DFC device would have induced them to leave the process of capital formation and allocation to these forces.

12.   Moreover, although the primary purpose of these early-model DFCs was term lending for industrial projects in the private sector, they were to promote and rationalize development in other ways also: by improving the appraisal methods of projects; by providing equity for especially worthy

projects; and by mobilizing long-term investment resources and fostering incipient capital markets through the sale of their own securities and their matured protfolio. It was expected that they would underwrite or guarantee private securities issues in some cases, and upgrade and enforce accountancy and financial reporting practices for their clients (and, by example, for the entire corporate sector). Finally, they were expected to improve management capabilities and practices through rigorous loan supervision and business advisory services; to provide reliable and practical policy advice to governments; and to train staff who could reinforce the management of other financial institutions. In sum, DFCs were to play a dynamic role in the financial sector by being a laboratory, an example, and a source of initiative that would facilitate the growth of a healthy, broadly based capital market.

13.   Needless to say, no DFC has achieved all these objectives. DFCs have been fairly consistently effective allocators of resources. Domestic funds are provided in most cases by a government or central bank; and external loans, often on concessional terms, come from multilateral and bilateral institutions. Lately, for some DFCs, loans on nonconcessional terms have come from the international banking network. A number of DFCs owe their existence to an initial World Bank commitment and continue to exist largely as favored channels for Bank financing, supplemented by the Asian, African, or Interamerican regional banks, the European Investment Bank (EIB); the OPEC or Arab funds; or bilateral aid. 3/ Such a limited role has a certain obvious utility in simplifying (or routinizing) the desirable transfer and national application of external resources, but it contributes little to the mobilization of domestic resources or to institutional development, as the next sections illustrate.

14.   In any event, DFCs <u>were</u> created in large numbers--at least one for virtually every emerging sovereign entity and sometimes, as in Brazil and India, scores--to serve different regions or specialized clienteles. A few function as apex institutions, allocating funds to second-tier DFCs and in some measure reviewing and coordinating their operations.

Private and State-owned DFCs Compared

15.   In the original conception of the World Bank--which was not the inventor of DFCs but has been their leading supporter for more than thirty years--the model DFC was privately owned and controlled, but it generally required a special sanction and concessional financing (subordinated low- or no-interest loans) from government. Leveraged by this quasi-equity, it was expected to earn its way with a lending rate of only a modest margin over the cost of money. The majority shareholders were domestic banks, insurance companies, or leading industrialists. Foreign institutions were encouraged to take up minority holdings, and the International Finance Corporation (IFC) was frequently a participant. This kind of ownership pattern was favored in the belief that the project appraisals and investment decisions of privately controlled institutions would likely be sounder and less politically motivated than those of government entities. Predictably, this supposition was disputed by proponents of socialism, and also by other development protagonists.

16.   Various grounds have been adduced for doubting the private DFC model:

●   <u>Viability</u>. Well managed DFCs in countries having a dynamic industrial economy can expect consistent earnings (as achieved, for example, by KDFC-KLB/Korea and most of the Colombian <u>financieras</u>). Nonetheless, their industrial term lending, especially to new or small enterprises, is generally unrewarding in comparison with other investment. Thus, many private investors funded the early-model DFCs not for direct profits but because of

institutional public relations, or the access they gained to a financial inner
circle, or the advantage they had in being at the head of the queue for term
loans. In addition, of course, their equity was highly leveraged by low-
interest government loans. Such inducements may not apply, or may not appeal
to the investors, in later capital increases.

● Availability of capital. Many countries (such as Bangladesh and most
of sub-Saharan Africa) simply lack sufficient private capital to fund an
effective DFC. To them, government ownership seems a necessary recourse. In
many cases this attitude is reinforced by ideological leanings.

● Economic vicissitudes. The industrial sector of the developing
countries has suffered many ups and downs over the past twenty years as a
result of payments crises, import restrictions, political upheavals,
nationalizations, price and credit controls, inflation, exchange fluctuations,
arbitrary interest rates, and so on. These factors have further threatened
the profitability, sometimes even the survival, of private DFCs.

● Susceptibility to influence. Although evidence is scanty, rumors are
rife about the inability of DFCs to resist certain pressures. Evidently
private ownership or control in itself cannot guarantee against government
pressures. Private as well as state-owned DFCs inevitably depend in many ways
on government favor or cooperation; and if powerful officials seek particular
loan approvals or other decisions--whether from political or personal motives
--the DFC may find it hard to resist. In addition, private DFCs are
susceptible to undue influence by "insiders," that is, the bankers or business
groups that frequently control them.

17.   One especially knowledgeable DFC practitioner, certainly not a socialist ideologue, contends that

> for engaging in real developmental activities, a development bank should be fully or substantially state-owned. . . .   The primary objective of a development bank by definition must be to strive for development . . . of the economy. Yet . . . no development bank can be oblivious to the profit motive . . . .Unlike a business enterprise, making the maximum possible profit may not be its obsession, yet it must make reasonable . . ., steady profits . . . to maintain its viability and carry out all the promotional activity requiring research and development. (Talwar 1982, pp. 4-5)

In many state-owned DFCs, however, concern for profitability is subordinated to other objectives; some officials (for example, a chairman of IDBI/India before Talwar) seem to consider it not quite respectable.

III. Attributes of State-owned and Private DFCs

18.   The World Bank opened its loan windows to governmental DFCs in 1968; several companies that had originally been largely private--for example, ICICI/India, PICIC/Pakistan, DBS/Singapore, DFCC/Sri Lanka, and NIDB/Nigeria --came effectively under state control. 4/ Today the great majority of DFCs in the developing world (excluding small commercial or household finance companies) are state owned, but they still lend mainly to the private sector. Most developing countries have also nationalized major components of the commercial banking system in order to eliminate foreign control and to make banks more responsive to public policy. The ownership pattern for other types of financial institutions varies: the longer established ones (such as mortgage banks and insurance companies) now tend to be state owned; the newer, often investor-oriented entities (securities firms, mutual funds, commercial finance and leasing companies) are more likely to be private.

19.   Not only do these various institutions have different purposes, market niches, and clienteles, but they are heavily influenced by differing national traditions, cultures, and economic environments. All these factors may override the state-private dichotomy. Still, certain generic distinctions can be recognized, as the following paragraphs show.

Extent of Governmental Influence

20.   State ownership is assumed to make DFCs more amenable to the government's purposes and priorities than private intermediaries would normally be. This assumption is plausible but hard to assess in practice. One reason is that the influence public authorities can exert may be little less for a private DFC (which is usually vested with a quasi-public character) than for a state-owned one (see para. 16 above). Moreover, since state-owned DFCs tend to be assigned multifarious objectives (which may be competitive or contradictory) without clear guidance as to priorities or trade-offs among them, the pursuit of one purpose may undercut another. The extent of overall conformity with governmental aims is therefore hard to determine.

21.   The degree or effect of governmental influence on DFCs cannot really be understood unless a distinction is made between the application of general policies and the pressures for specific investment decisions. As for the latter, a distinction must also be made between official purposes and those of special, perhaps corrupt, interests. Such interests surely exist, but their prevalence is not susceptible to systematic analysis. Usually they are successfully concealed by all parties and treated gingerly by the media and juridical authorities. Occasionally a chief executive resigns in protest but does not publicize the reason. In any case, there are no data indicating the incidence of improper governmental pressures on state-owned or private DFCs. Certain characteristics of private companies (for example, their

decisionmaking procedures are less open to public scrutiny, they may feel less secure as nongovernmental entities, and their profits might suffer from official hostility) suggest that they may be even more vulnerable to such pressures than state-owned institutions. Evidence to support this conjecture, however, is scant and inconclusive.

22.   As might be expected, government-directed financing for specific projects is better documented and more common among state-owned than private DFCs. In the Republic of Korea, for instance, government-directed loans for specific projects in 1976-78 accounted for more than 50 percent of lending by the banking system (almost wholly state owned) and an even greater proportion of lending by the parastatal DFCs, especially KDB; BNDE/Brazil, also instructed by the government, initially concentrated on financing railways, later electric power, and still later iron and steel and other basic industrial projects identified in the National Plan. More recently it has financed small and medium enterprise (SME), which is less easily pinpointed and therefore reflects a policy emphasis rather than any particular project. Despite their commitments, in a typical charter or policy statement, to managerial autonomy and investment integrity, many state-owned DFCs have been persuaded to fund favored projects which may or may not meet normal appraisal criteria. 5/ Still, these commitments give DFCs a certain bargaining power, enabling them to insist on a proper feasibility study for a state-sponsored project, or to negotiate changes to improve its viability, or occasionally to stall it indefinitely. (This bargaining strength may be reinforced by the concerns and conditions of external lenders. 6/) Sometimes such review is welcomed by finance or planning officials who would like, but are unable on their own, to delay or kill a project having strong support from politicians or operating departments. In other cases, however, the central finance and

planning agencies may be the principal forces pressing a DFC to satisfy a specific government demand. Such ambiguities characterize governments everywhere. Thus, well-managed and well-staffed state-owned DFCs may often introduce a second opinion in the decisionmaking process on investment proposals favored by the government of the day. That opinion is often overridden, but it may lead to reconsideration. And while not infallible, of course, it should reflect rational, consistent criteria and professional competence.

23.   Private DFCs, on the other hand, are seldom given open directives to finance specific projects; but they may be subject to subtle pressures since they often consult with the authorities, know well the latter's wishes, and want to maintain cordial relations. The weight of such factors in questionable loan or investment decisions by private DFCs is not measurable, evinced only in confidential reports and rumors. Occasionally DFCs are delegated responsibility for managing a government's investments with a view to insulating them from political influence, but the DFCs so charged are normally state owned. Only one private DFC--IMDBI/Iran--was so entrusted; and in this role, of course, it was subject to government direction.

Coordinating Role

24.   Some DFCs, while administering their own operational programs, also coordinate the allocation of resources to other institutions. Outstanding examples are IDBI/India and BNDE/Brazil, both in countries of exceptional size and diversity, and DBP/Philippines. Although all three are state owned, they finance mainly private sector enterprises.

25.   IDBI was the last of India's nationwide state financial institutions to be created but now is the most important. Apart from directly financing large (mostly private) projects, it coordinates national development financing

and channels resources (external and domestic) to the numerous state finance corporations and state industrial development corporations; the former assist some large projects of special regional importance but mainly assist small-scale enterprises. IDBI is represented on the board of directors of each state-owned DFC (all except ICICI are state owned). It is an important shareholder in all the above-mentioned state corporations, sits on their boards, and conducts an annual review of their financial and operational programs. In addition, it chairs periodic meetings of all the state DFCs to determine how the financing of certain major projects will be shared and to decide issues of policy or common interest. It also participates in similar coordination meetings of the major commercial banks convened by the Reserve Bank of India. Thus IDBI is explicitly an agent of government policy. Its board of directors is appointed by government and overlaps that of the Reserve Bank; at least half of IDBI's board, however, comes from the private sector.

26.   The kingpin of government-sponsored programs for the promotion and financing of economic development in Brazil is BNDE, established in 1952. At first, as noted in para. 22, it financed railways, electric power, and iron and steel projects; later, while continuing to finance iron and steel, it emphasized other basic industries. From 1966 BNDE took the lead in developing the National System of Development Banks, which is made up of twenty-four institutions in which BNDE holds equity shares, and to which it allocates resources from several federal funds on the basis of an annual joint program review. This relationship enables BNDE to help direct and ensure the financing of government-mandated projects of changing priority. It also allows BNDE to decentralize decisionmaking so that regional needs can be served effectively and the geographic concentration of industry mitigated.

The resources channeled through subsidiary DFCs are still a small proportion of BNDE's total financing, but the percentage is increasing.

27.　　DBP/Philippines, meanwhile, combines the functions of a conventional DFC (it administers a number of government programs to foster development of specific economic sectors or regions) and an apex institution (it channels funds to a network of commercial and rural banks). These roles are less far-reaching than those of IDBI or BNDE, however.

28.　　In coordinating government development policy, each of these DFCs oversees (and helps to finance) the operations of various national or regional intermediaries. Others, like KDB in Korea, are instruments for external borrowing and for the allocation of funds to designated industrial subsectors and to other intermediaries serving specialized clienteles (such as SMI). All these institutions are state owned and controlled; no private institution, given its conflicting interests, would likely be entrusted with decisions of this type.

29.　　Many senior executives of private DFCs, however, are valued counselors to government. Because of their personal prestige, their linkages to both business and development interests, and their ability to bring micro issues to the attention of the macro planners, they are often consulted on industrial and financial matters. The chairman of ICICI, for example, is a member of the Central Industrial Advisory Council of India. The managing director of IMDBI/Iran was not only entrusted with the management of the large government investment portfolio and promotional funds, but also was the principal adviser and protagonist in the development of Iran's stock exchange, other capital market institutions, and supporting (including regulatory) mechanisms. The chairman of KDFC-KLB/Korea and the presidents of PDFC/Philippines and of the principal South American financieras are all financial elder statesmen in their respective countries and constantly provide behind-the-scenes advice to the authorities.

Resource Mobilization

30.   In general, all DFCs have three basic functions: to attract external resources, to mobilize domestic savings, and to allocate both in a rational fashion. Most DFCs have achieved the first objective in substantial measure --that is, they are usually the favored channels for loans from public international or bilateral sources. Some are also preferred borrowers for world-class banks, within credit limits set for the country. Several countries (for example, Indonesia, Korea, and the Philippines) have been increasingly reluctant to guarantee international loans for private DFCs; if it became routine, such a policy would cut off these DFCs from their accustomed World Bank, regional development bank, and official bilateral sources. At the same time, these countries have continued to seek such financing for their state-owned institutions. The World Bank normally resists such discrimination; nevertheless it may set as a condition of its lending that the DFC must raise matching funds from other (mainly private) sources (for example, Ecuador, Morocco, Turkey). The private DFCs are thus under continuing pressure to diversify their sources of foreign funding.

31.   As for the second objective, the record of DFCs in mobilizing domestic resources is mixed, but poor on the whole for both private and state-owned DFCs, particularly for the latter. Government institutions, by and large, are not concerned with the availability of domestic resources because they draw on the national budget or the central bank for whatever sums their approved lending targets require, often at concessional rates. 7/ Private DFCs generally have to compete for private funds on commercial terms. They have found it increasingly difficult to do so, since rising inflation and

payments deficits have pushed up interest rates and constrained bank credits. 8/
Inflation has also eroded the equity base of private and state-owned DFCs
alike. As a result, new infusions of capital are required to support a
growing volume (at least in nominal terms) of lending. For the state-owned
companies, however, the need for increased capital is less pressing, since the
public treasury ultimately guarantees their solvency. 9/

32.   Understandably in the circumstances, state-owned DFCs have been less
active and innovative than their private counterparts in mobilizing domestic
resources, especially in the market. State-owned DFCs have little compulsion
or incentive to woo private funds so long as they can count on public money to
meet contingencies. That reliance may be illusory, in view of other growing
claims on a straitened budget. In Brazil, for example, the rapid expansion of
public funding ended abruptly for BNDE in 1978. Despite a tenfold increase in
time deposits (from a very low base), its resources are still far below those
projected. Other state-owned DFCs have suffered similar problems; those like
KDB/Korea, which had begun to tap private savings before the budgetary crunch,
have adjusted better.

33.   Private DFCs faced earlier and more severe problems in mobilizing
term resources, which they sought to counter in various ways even as the
difficulties mounted. KDFC/Korea, established in 1966 on the model then
sponsored by the World Bank, was converted in 1980 into the Korea Long Term
Credit Bank (KLB), patterned after a successful Japanese institution. It is
still privately owned but has more than tripled its paid-in capital and has
floated a large bond issue, greatly aided by the high regard it enjoys in the
business community. Its leasing, securities, and short-term finance
subsidiaries also bolstered its profits--at least until the recent
recession. In the Philippines, meanwhile, PDCP and PISO have gone farther in

diversification, linking up with commercial banks (whose deposits are most useful) and also undertaking securities, money market, and consultancy activities. In Colombia the regional financieras have obtained necessary accretions of equity through their close relationship with the business elite. Although they have mobilized substantial sums through time deposits and short-term notes, persistent inflation and interest ceilings have impeded these efforts. As a result, some two-thirds of their total resources still derive from external borrowing and credit lines from the central bank. The Colombian, and even more the Ecuadorian, financieras use primarily domestic currency for short-term business and rely on foreign resources (from the World Bank and private banks) for longer term projects.

Range of Functions and Emphasis

34.   As was noted earlier, DFC operations are diversified in degree and in purpose. Most sub-Saharan African institutions are relatively young; deal with less-advanced economies; and, with few exceptions, are state owned. They continue generally to stick to their central function. In East Asia, however, various initiatives have emerged in response to the opportunities and needs created by the region's dynamism, to government wishes, and to growing financial vicissitudes. Private companies--such as KLB/Korea, PDCP and PISO/Philippines, and DBS/Singapore--have generally been more innovative and successful than state-owned DFCs in this regard.

35.   Some DFCs chose, were required, or were created specifically to serve a distinct clientele: a particular economic sector, SSE, parastatal companies, and so on. In most countries such specialzation has been mandated by government and the institutions are state owned. At the same time, a number of private DFCs have found it expedient to build up their competence to serve the needs of a particular economic constituency: for example, PDCP has

focused on SSE in the outlying regions of the Philippines; IMDBI on the sugar industry and its by-products in Iran; KDFC/Korea on fisheries, shipping, and electronics; and PICIC/Pakistan on the textile and jute industries. Their initiatives might have been motivated by politics or public relations, by concessional resources offered from the government or central bank, or by the prospect of new business down the road.

36.   Small-scale Enterprise. Many state-owned DFCs are assigned the function of lending for SSE; now and then such lending is also undertaken through special units of private companies such as PDCP/Philippines. Commercial banks, too, are increasingly funding SSE under special incentive-guarantee programs. SSE lending is more arduous and expensive per unit than financing on a larger scale. To be successful, it must be spread over a much greater number of scattered units, and decisionmaking must be more decentralized than is usual for DFCs, although not for commercial banks. SSE lending puts less emphasis on collateral and more on judging project merit, personal qualities, and potential cash flows, as is customary in DFC methodology. It follows streamlined procedures and simple criteria that draw on, but extend, both DFC and commercial bank traditions.

37.   State programs for SSE promotion tend to be loosely administered in most countries, which argue that small firms are financially fragile, short of working capital, and poor at bookeeping. High class financial performance, it is said, cannot be expected of them, and the inferior performance of which they are capable should not be hampered by stringent conditions. They are also credited with political clout, which makes the imposition of such conditions futile and their enforcement hazardous. These impressions are certainly exaggerated, but they reinforce the widely held view that SSE loans are really giveaways (or honeypots for "influential persons," as in the Kenya

Industrial Estates (KIE) program), and they provide a self-serving rationale
for lax follow-up. Obviously, private DFCs (which may show special favor to
powerful clients, as mentioned earlier, but surely not to SSEs) are less
subject to such vitiating perceptions and pressures. Wide variations are
evident, however, in the performance of state-owned institutions. Korea's
SMIB and CNB (the latter caters to mini-enterprises) have had almost no
arrears. In Kenya, 93 percent of KIE's loans were recently reported in
arrears over three months and this trend appears to be rising. On the other
hand, the Kenya Commercial Bank (also state owned), under an IFC-assisted
program for a target group of slightly larger size, has no persistent
arrears. Likewise, the state-owned Bank of Ceylon had no arrears in another
IFC project whereas the same bank, under a government-sponsored SSE program,
collected less than one-third of the amounts due from its borrowers, while a
private bank in the same program collected 72 percent. These differences
evidently relate in part to the country and its cultural environment, as in
Korea. Institutional traditions or attitudes also play a role, as they have
in the relatively better performance of the commercial banks (albeit state
owned) as against aid-oriented government programs. Perhaps SSE programs are
most influenced by the degree of seriousness shown and discipline sustained in
loan follow-up.

38.   Parastatals. Most private DFCs refuse to lend money to firms that
are wholly or predominantly state owned, but many accept projects in which
government holds a small share. Most state-owned DFCs finance government
projects (TIB/Tanzania gives them priority), but their credits go
preponderantly to the private sector. Parastatal projects are generally
funded through the national budget; but supplementary financing is sometimes
needed, and the national DFC may appear to be a convenient reserve. Within

the state-owned DFCs, although private and parastatal projects are said to be appraised and supervised according to the same criteria and methodology, their treatment inevitably differs in some respects. For one thing, official sponsorship ensures priority consideration. For another, the burden of proof for rejection rests on the DFC. Also, overzealous loan supervision may cause repercussions. Negotiations often replace, at all stages, the unilateral decision imposed on most private clients.

39.   Sectoral Emphases. Government generally mandates sectoral emphases, which are pursued by state-owned institutions under instruction and accepted with reservations by their private counterparts. That was the case, for example, in BNDE/Brazil's push for railways, then electric power, then steel; KDB/Korea's commitment to heavy metallurgy, machinery, and chemicals in the late 1970s; India's programs for rehabilitating "sick" industries; and the campaigns of DBP/Philippines to develop fisheries and treecrops. Some private companies have also identified and studied potentially dynamic sectors and fostered projects therein. KDFC/Korea, for example, has emphasized fishing vessels (long-line tuna boats and trawlers), which generated numerous loans both to domestic fisheries and for export of Korean equipment, and the purchase of second-hand cargo ships for a rapid and cheap expansion of the Korean fleet, which earned foreign exchange and promoted employment of Koreans in both national and foreign shipping. In addition, Korea has emphasized electronics production, for which a special government program of technological enhancement has been established, and machine-building, where government support has been focused on production of precision equipment. The Colombian financieras, in recent years, have analyzed the country's export potential and stressed financing of industries contributing thereto.

40.   Promotion. Most DFCs are content to deal with project proposals that are brought to them by outside sponsors, whether private entrepreneurs or government agencies. Some, however, have assumed an independent promotional role by actively studying the potential of certain industrial sectors, seeking out viable project designs, commissioning feasibility studies, locating suitable technical partners, working up appropriate financial packages and enlisting necessary support, choosing key management personnel, and overseeing all stages of the process. It is an important process, often glamorous and exciting, but beset with unforseeable difficulties.

41.   Gasem Kheradjou, former chief executive of IMBDI/Iran (the DFC most notably active in the promotion of large enterprises), has described some of these difficulties in a paper prepared for the Economic Development Institute (1982). He notes, for example, numerous deficiencies in the performance of IMDBI's foreign partners, technological and commercial, as well as opposition from Iranian vested interests. Nonetheless, IMDBI was the principal patron and administrator of numerous key enterprises in Iran, largely because of its best-of-both-worlds relationship with the Iranian government. It enjoyed close rapport and governmental support (including some $250 million of state funds entrusted to IMDBI's management), yet had private sector flexibility and freedom of action. Several large projects it promoted initially had only three shareholders: government, IMDBI, and a foreign partner. This tripartite pattern avoided both government control, which was uncomfortable for the foreign participant, and foreign control, which was unacceptable to the government. Once IMDBI was well established, the government issued a number of important industrial project licences to it rather than to individual sponsors. Thus, the projects did not have to be restricted to a single investment group and a broader range of investors could be enlisted.

Furthermore, IMDBI's private character helped to reassure potential investors, both domestic and foreign.

42.   Another notably entrepreneurial DFC is the state-owned BDC/Botswana, which has launched several companies (among them, a brewery that is very large by the scale of the Botswana economy) to take advantage of its customs union with South Africa. BDC acts explicitly as an executive arm of the government, substituting for an entrepreneurial class capable of undertaking large-scale projects; such a class is virtually nonexistent among the indigenous people. BDC's ventures have prospered, by and large. PDCP/Philippines and KLB/Korea also actively seek projects of willing entrepreneurs, preferring not to be primary sponsors themselves. DBM/Mauritius, meanwhile, promotes and administers industrial estates.

43.   A few companies in other countries have created new enterprises, frequently to their subsequent regret. It is a difficult and risky business. Such an undertaking preempts the scarcest DFC resources: equity capital (elementary prudence warns against using medium-term borrowed funds to finance the equity base in new, untested companies) and top executive manpower. In addition, it involves complex technological, management, and marketing decisions that are outside the DFC's normal range of competence. And, although the rewards may be substantial, they are uncertain and usually long delayed.

44.   Capital Market Development. From their inception, DFCs were expected to contribute importantly to the growth and institutionalization of securities markets:

●   By floating their own relatively long-term bonds or notes designed to meet the objectives of different savers;

●   By creating and eventually selling portfolio securities representing successful firms funded by them;

• By imposing loan supervision and accounting or audit requirements for
enterprises they were financing, thus providing a model for upgrading the
standards of financial reporting in general;

• By requiring their borrowers, sometimes, to go public;

• By forming subsidiaries to deal in securities and to create a
secondary market.

45.   The results, over the thirty-year span of DFC experience, have been
mixed, mostly disappointing. Although the development of capital markets is
often included among government policy objectives, it is seldom given high
priority in the absence of strong pressure from the private sector. The
private sector is usually more concerned with immediate grievences--interest
rates, price controls, import restrictions--than with long-range institution
building of a nature and complexity that are imperfectly understood by either
government or most private managers. In this kind of situation, an
experienced DFC may be able to play a crucial role as an informed interlocutor
between government and the business and financial community.

46.   Thus, IMDBI persuaded the government to amend the law for the
protection of minority shareholders in companies, and to provide certain tax
incentives for listing and trading in the stock exchange. It helped to draft
new company and stock exchange laws; and it studied the rules and procedures
of small exchanges around the world and drafted regulations for the new Tehran
Stock Exchange, of which the managing director was elected chairman (he also
sponsored the establishment of a school of business administration). IMDBI
also persuaded Iran's largest commercial bank (state owned) to promote the
sale of shares through its branch network; and in conjunction with this bank
and Merrill Lynch, it organized a brokerage firm. Elsewhere, KLB/Korea set up
subsidiaries for underwriting securities, to issue and trade in short-term

instruments and to meet temporary cash requirements of business firms, and for industrial leasing; its own successful flotation of bonds constitutes a breakthrough in nongovernment issues. DBS/Singapore has evolved into a sort of financial supermarket, while PDCP/Philippines has formed underwriting and securities-trading subsidiaries. Since a well-developed financial sector already existed in the Philippines, it had less occasion than IMDBI/Iran to intervene with government. IFCI/India underwrites share issues as part of its financing package. The Colombian financieras also have contributed substantially to capital market development.

47.   Except for IFCI, the DFCs cited above are private. They look to the capital markets to raise most of their domestic resources, through bond or note issues and turnover of their investment portfolios. They frequently need to enlist institutional investors to cofinance, refinance, or eventually sell projects, to explore and combine various alternatives, and to negotiate keenly on prices and margins rather than merely respond to government directives and rely on government funding. Thus, private DFCs have the self-interest and incentive to play an active role in promoting the development of a strong, varied, and buoyant capital market. State-owned DFCs have less need for market resources or incentive to refinance or sell their investments. Exceptions in some degree are two nationalized commercial banks, in Kenya and Sri Lanka, which are becoming more development oriented and have established merchant banking affiliates; both are assisted by IFC.

48.   Consultancy Services. The value of well-trained advisors who can offer practical services to small and medium entrepreneurs embarking on new types of production--not only in matters of technology but more generally on marketing, inventory control, financial planning, and other aspects of business management--is widely recognized. But delivery of such services in a

systematic, economical, and professionally competent fashion has proved difficult. Government-sponsored industrial or business extension units usually find it hard to attract adequately qualified staff. They also have difficulty establishing their credibility with clients, and building up a mutually reinforcing relationship with financial institutions. In several countries, therefore, financial institutions have set up their own consultancy affiliates. Most of these are linked to state-owned DFCs--SMIB/Korea and IDBI/India are notable examples--but perhaps the most ambitious and successful is Asian Business Consultants (ABC), a subsidiary of PDCP/Philippines.

49.   ABC carries on a varied program of: assistance to turn around companies in trouble, through redirection of corporate strategy, reorganization of management, and actually running the business for at least two years; sectoral and other economic research studies; specific studies of corporate prospects, job evaluation, project feasibility, management systems, and the like; executive recruitment, on commission; management training and development, stressing an adaptation of Japanese approaches to problem solving; and entrepreneurship training, which was recently introduced. ABC is self-supporting and serves both corporate and governmental clients. It undoubtedly has greater impact and success as a private sector enterprise than it would as a government agency. Its public as well as private clients are mainly concerned with, and need a realistic understanding of, private industrial-financial activity. ABC also reinforces PDCP's in-service training programs and the courses it organizes (with UNDP and World Bank support) for the Asia/Pacific regional association of DFCs.

50.   KLB/Korea's consultancy programs are less ambitious, and are largely for borrowers rather than business in general. They relate to financing possibilities and contracts, intermediation of finance and technology

transfers, organization of joint ventures, and feasibility studies for underwriting mergers and new projects. ICICI, India's only DFC with a private tradition, sponsors just one of the thirteen regional organizations of technical consultants established under the national leadership of IDBI. These organizations conduct preparatory studies of various kinds: they anlyze the industrial potential of a state or district; identify projects and assess their feasibility; review project design or appraisal reports; and so on. Since 1973, the State Bank of India has developed a system of consultancy service cells to strengthen management capabilities in its SSE clients and to improve the bank's own skills and project assessments for SSE financing. A few other commercial banks in India have taken similar initiatives on a smaller scale.

51.   A key feature of several IFC projects designed to finance small- and (mainly) medium-scale industries through commercial bank intermediaries is that they have established business advisory services (BAS) within the local bank. Some of the intermediaries (including the one in Kenya, where the BAS unit has been conspicuously successful so far) are state owned, but their support of the BAS concept is a significant departure from their recent private banking origin. Their willingness to make such a departure, and that of India's banks mentioned above, may be attributed perhaps to their perception of the potential economic or commercial advantage of BAS, perhaps to the increased public service obligations implied by their nationalization, or perhaps to a fortunate concurrence of both. At any rate, in the few contexts that permit comparison, these BAS units have a better record of performance and a better reputation for practical utility than the parallel government services.

Performance

52.   Operating Ratios. The latest compilation available for a large
sample of DFCs is for the period 1977-79. Its value for comparing operational
efficiency is open to question. The sample comprises fifty-three
institutions; the African, EMENA, and East Asia regions are well represented
(albeit only 1979 figures are available for much of Africa), but Colombia is
overweighted in Latin America and only Bangladesh and Pakistan are represented
in South Asia. The ratios presented are: (1) gross income, (2) administrative
expenses, and (3) financial expenses, each as percentage of average total
assets for the year; (4) administrative expense/number of professional staff;
(5) dividends and capital gains/average equity portfolio; (6) loan
income/average portfolio; (7) volume of approvals/number of professional
staff; (8) cost of debt/average debt; (9) net profits, and (10) pretax
earnings, both as a percentage of average net worth. The comparisons within
and between these categories are discussed briefly in the paragraphs that
follow, and the tabulation is attached as Annex A.

53.   Item (1) above must be related to (3), which is largely a function of
interest rates in the respective countries but is also affected by
concessional finance from governments and by the particular DFC's financial
structure. The gross income ratios are generally much higher for Colombia's
financieras than for the DFCs of any other region. Their financial expense
ratios are also high, but their net margin in 1979 averaged about 7.5 percent
as against a crude worldwide average for all fifty-three companies of about
4.75 percent. The difference in both cost of money and margin presumably
reflected market assessment of inflation. Profitability of the private DFCs
of Colombia (as measured by pretax earnings/average net worth) was also much
higher, in the 20-40 percent range, than for companies in other regions (with

the notable exception of IDBI/Israel, where a still greater inflation rate inflated nominal profits).

54.   In Ecuador and Bolivia, the margins were smaller (especially for CFN, Ecuador's state-owned DFC, although its cost of debt was lower than that of its principal private competitor, COFIEC). In East Asia the margins ranged from a high of 5.2-6.3 percent over the three years for CDC/Taiwan, to lows of 2.7-2.5 percent for DBP/Philippines, with a crude average of 4.3 percent for 1979. The margins for the EMENA institutions listed were all in the range of 2-3 percent, except in Israel (where margins ranged from -1.4 percent in 1977 to 4.8 percent in 1979, reflecting inflation and adaptation thereto) and in Ireland (where the average was about 4 percent). Both these countries reported a relatively high cost of debt. The four South Asian DFCs all had margins around (mostly below) 3 percent.

55.   The picture for Africa in 1979 was still less consistent. BDC/Botswana's margin between the gross income and cost of money ratios was 11.5 percent as against an average of 5 percent for the entire sample from Africa, and its pretax earnings were 25.1 percent of net worth (mainly attributable to its large equity investments and an extraordinary capital gain from the sale of one of them). DBZ/Zambia and SOFIDE/Zaire (a private company) enjoyed margins of 9.1 percent and 8.4 percent, respectively, between items (1) and (3); and SOFIDE had pretax earnings of 20 percent, aided by an exceptionally low average cost of debt. NIB/Ghana also had a relatively high gross income minus financial expense margin (7.9 percent) and 27 percent earnings for the single year reported (1979), despite a relatively high cost of debt, which was probably due to a low debt/net worth ratio. At the other extreme, SOFISEDIT/Senegal had a declining margin which was negative by 4.8 percent in 1979; and it lost 28 percent of net worth in that year.

56.   Administrative expense as a percentage of total assets (item 2) and per number of professional staff (item 4) has a bearing on the volume of approvals per staff numbers (item 7). These ratios relate to operational efficiency, but also reflect a number of other factors. For one, salary scales (converted to U.S. dollars) are high in certain West African countries and include substantial expatriate participation, whereas scales are predictably low in South Asia. Some incipient (and sluggish) DFCs, such as IBS/Sudan, have an inordinately low volume of approvals. SSE institutions, such as CFP/Colombia and CNB/Korea, have a designedly low unit value of loans. As well, a high proportion of large parastatal projects call for little appraisal or supervision relative to their size (on the part of TIB/Tanzania or KDB/Korea). In East Asia, as in Colombia, the highest administrative expense ratios are for the state-owned DFCs serving specifically small and medium enterprises--CNB and SMIB/Korea (both state-owned). Meanwhile, KDFC (now KLB)/Korea) has consistently been lowest. But for volume of approvals relative to professional staffing, SMIB is among the leaders; its rank is a tribute to operational streamlining.

57.   Computerization. Increasing use of computer techniques for management information, communications, and a variety of routine operations seems an inevitable trend for larger DFCs, even in low-wage countries, especially for those decentralizing to a substantial extent. PDFC/Philippines has for some time been progressively computerizing its payments to creditors and shareholder loan disbursements, client obligations and payments, personnel and payroll actions (including paychecks), internal accounts, financial projections on behalf of prospective borrowers, and (underway) comprehensive financial projections for PDFC itself. The processes of hardware selection, programs development, and training of operators have been telescoped to

overlap in time in order to put the system into operation as quickly as possible.

58.   KLB/Korea started the computerization process with a consultants' feasibility study in 1978. It also formulated a phased plan extending beyond 1984, of which implementation is well underway. In India, the State Bank has computerized its operations extensively, but IDBI continues with mainly manual operations, apparently to preserve clerical jobs. This seems a questionable policy, from a standpoint not so much of employment as of accessibility, continuity, and timeliness of management information and records. But computerization strategy—objectives, phasing, and choice of equipment and programs—needs to be studied carefully in light of a DFC's specific requirements before commitments are made.

59.   Collections. One significant measure of a DFC's operational performance is the proportion of timely collections of the amounts of principal and interest due to it—or, on the other side of the coin, the proportion of arrears and defaults. Unfortunately, meaningful comparative statistics for a substantial number of DFCs, both private and public sector institutions, are hard to come by. Intercountry comparisons are often distorted by differing cultural traditions and legal systems; and within countries different areas of institutional specialization (by sector or clientele) or differing policies on loan rescheduling may affect the collection record. All the Korean institutions, for example, have almost no arrears; CNB has recently been concerned that the amounts that are ninety days overdue have risen (presumably because of economic recession) from 0.7 percent to 1.1 percent. In Indonesia, BAPINDO recently reduced its arrears rate to only 1.5 percent by dint of extensive rescheduling, while PDFCI's rose to 7.5 percent, largely because of ill-fated money market activity. Overdues for

some of the African DFCs are more than 50 percent. (Para. 37 discusses the experience in a few SSE lending programs.)

60.   _Profitability_. Almost all DFCs are supposed to be financially self-sustaining and to show a profit, and in the years 1977-1979 most of them did so, in widely varying degree. In countries where comparison is possible, private companies were typically more profitable (see Annex A). For example, in the late 1970s the private institution COFIEC/Ecuador had pretax earnings (as a percentage of net worth) four to five times those of the state-owned CFN, which actually sustained a net loss in 1979. In Korea during the same years the ratio for KDFC (private) was 26-28 percent, as against 4-9 percent for KDB and SMIB, but a startling 32.7 percent for CNB because its net worth is very small in relation to its operations and total assets. In Colombia, meanwhile, the private _financieras_ consistently earned 25-40 percent of net worth, whereas CFP rose from 2 percent in 1977 to 11.3 percent in 1979, still negative in real terms. In the Philippines, DBP's earnings of about 5 percent contrast with those of 14-25 percent for PDCP and PISO. And in Indonesia BAPINDO (state) earned 3-4 percent as against PDFCI's (private) 6.5-9.5 percent. The subsequent experience of PDFCI was less favorable, as high arrears turned into losses. SOFISEDIT/Senegal was an exception, as it experienced consistent and severe losses.

61.   Privately owned DFCs naturally pursue profits more assiduously. Their lives depend on their profits. But managers of state-owned institutions also have a considerable stake in profitability. It enhances their standing with and also their independence from their governmental masters, and helps to ensure their continued tenure or advancement. It also enables them to fulfill their developmental mission with greater resources and lower financial costs. Hence managers of DFCs, public or private, need to protect reasonable

profit margins. Private managers may be somewhat more determined and ingenious in doing so, and less affected by the often contrary inclinations of the political authorities; but they are no less plagued by inflation and interest ceilings, and they generally have to pay more for their money. Their relative performance is thus worthy of note.

Services and Benefits to Clients

62.   The banker-client relationship is stereotypically ambivalent. The bank is a vital ally, a crutch for the necessitous borrower; but it is an avaricious bloodsucker when the loan repayment date finds the borrower in financial straits. DFCs were designed to be more understanding, patient, and supportive than their commercial counterparts--and by and large they have been so. The average term and grace period of their loans are longer and thus ease the payment burden during a project's infancy. Their loan supervision often contributes substantially to a resolution of problems as well as to the collection of overdues--although performance in both regards varies widely. The objective of institutional profit is diluted, sometimes submerged, by national development purposes.

63.   In comparing the client services and benefits of private and state-owned DFCs, one must distinguish between conventional and explicitly SSE-oriented institutions, the latter being usually state owned. To be successful, these SSE banks have to devote a great deal of attention to technical assistance, often of a rather elementary kind. That assistance may require a disproportionate expenditure of resources relative to that of the conventional DFC but is often reinforced or subsidized by the government. State-owned companies predominate in this area.

64.   A much larger share of DFC lending, however, goes to larger firms, which may be financed, in different countries, from governmental or private

sources or both--preponderantly government in South Asia, Korea, Indonesia, and most of Africa; largely private in northern South America; and quite mixed in Brazil and the Philippines. State-owned DFCs usually offer the more favorable loan terms for projects that conform to government priorities. Ancillary services tend to be provided more by private DFCs in countries with a mixed banking system (see paragraphs 34 and 48-51). An important difference, although hard to define or measure, is the degree of psychological rapport with the business community. Now and then, the chief executives of state-owned DFCs are drawn from that community and expect to return to it; but more usually they are politicians or civil servants, and their principal asociates have the same background. Although businessmen may respect and cultivate these public DFC managers, given a choice they are likely to feel more attuned to those of private-sector institutions. The enduring old boy network of the Colombian financieras and their clients, and that of Pakistan's industrial oligarchy up to the mid-1970s, are examples of financial symbiosis.

Staff Compensation and Continuity

65.   Private DFCs consistently have an advantage in attracting and retaining professional staff. Although autonomous parastatal institutions are often not strictly subject to civil service salaries, their scales are not fully equivalent to commercial scales; and their employment security and pension entitlements are devalued by inflation. Thus, experienced personnel in state-owned DFCs are frequently lured into the private sector at home or abroad. The public institutions in these countries provide a nursery for financial expertise and thereby help to nourish financial sector development, 10/ but in the process they may lose the best of their senior professionals and be left with the dregs and novices. By the same token, staff continuity and career progression in private DFCs such as KLB/Korea, PDCP/Philippines, TSKB/Turkey,

and so on, have been important contributors to the success of these institutions.

Organization and Management Style

66.   The organizational patterns of financial institutions are not primarily determined by public as opposed to private ownership. Yet this factor may have a significant influence on several aspects of organizational structure.

* The relative importance of different functions, and hence the status and authority given to the departments responsible. State-owned DFCs, for example, commonly assign a lower priority to resource mobilization, except in attracting deposits. Thus, the securities marketing unit may be small or nonexistent, and low in the managerial hierarchy. Or SSE development, usually state sponsored, may be given a starring role. Or a private DFC may stress aggressive business development, as do PDCP and PISO/Philippines, KLB/Korea, and the South American financieras. Or it may engage heavily in short-term money market operations, as do these financieras and PDFCI/Indonesia.

* Directorate. The official membership of the policymaking boards of most state-owned DFCs is diluted by some representation from the private sector or from independent public interest groups (as in BNDE/Brazil, IDBI and ICICI/India, SMIB/Korea). Some DFCs (such as BNDE and SMIB) have a two-tier directorate, with a second working board for day-to-day operations composed of top management personnel. Occasionally the two are melded into a mixed policy-operating board combining official-inside-outside representation (DBP/Philippines). The combination of these disparate influences in the policy direction of a DFC seems desirable. But, as an instrument for direction of day-to-day operations, the external participation is of dubious value unless all members have a long-term commitment to their supervisory role

and tenure (as is apparently intended for DBP) and can work well together. Many private DFCs (such as the regional financieras in Colombia, COFIEC/Ecuador, PDCP/Philippines, IMDBI/Iran until 1979, and ICICI/India and KDFC-KLB/Korea until recently) have been molded in large part by a single individual, who has continued to have a dominant voice in policymaking and operational direction. Hence, their administrative pyramid comes to a sharp apex, at which stands the "old man" or, increasingly now, his anointed successor.

● Delegation and span of control. In state-owned DFCs, the delegation of effective responsibility tends to be greater than in private DFCs because chief executives change more often. The second-level staff must be relied on for continuity. This pattern is consistent with the working directorate cited above, which considers operational policy issues in collegial fashion but leaves implementation to a particular director in charge. However, one of the largest DFCs, IDBI/India, has a single board chairman/managing director at the top and only three executive directors (two until recently) at the next managerial level, each of whom is responsible for several departments that carry out a wide range of representational, policy coordination, advisory, and consultancy functions; or deal with nearly $1 billion of direct loan approvals and a greater volume of branch or indirect (SFCs under IDBI supervision) operations; or administer a variety of staff functions; or mobilize domestic and overseas resources on an increasing scale; or handle several of the foregoing categories. IDBI's delegation of responsibility from the chairman to the next level is substantial, but at that level the managerial pyramid seem too narrow. Managerial control is also highly concentrated in the private DFCs of South America and East Asia, but with two differences: first, their financing volume and economic impact are far less than IDBI's; and, second, the chief executives are founding fathers or permanent fixtures rather than transitory political appointees.

● Geographical concentration or dispersion. Most DFCs, unlike commercial banks, tend to cluster their staff resources and decisionmaking at headquarters or in a few branch offices. The principal exceptions are DFCs primarily or substantially concerned with SSE development, and these, as has been noted earlier, are preponderantly state owned. Other factors as well make for a more dispersed branch network in state-owned DFCs compared with private DFCs: the former have a greater propensity for delegation, as noted earlier; they tend to rely on detailed rules and procedures, whereas many private DFCs have a more personal style of management; they are generally less concerned about the administrative expense of a branch network, relative to the public relations advantage of a local presence; and they are often assigned, by government directive, certain location-related functions (fisheries, treecrops, development of backward areas, and the like). Thus, decentralization, with its many implications for the DFC's structure, administrative costs, and efficiency and relationships with clients, may not be the result of management's weighing of the alternatives and trade-offs, but rather of government mandate or pressures. This is not a criticism, merely a recognition of reality.

IV. Summary and Conclusions

67.   The foregoing discussion has shown that DFCs come in many shapes and sizes, and that their mode and efficiency of management are influenced by numerous factors. State or private ownership is one such factor, but evidently it is not often predominant. Cultural traditions, social

organization, the politicoeconomic environment, and personal attitudes may well be more significant. Still, some tentative generalizations seem worthy of mention.

Comparisons

68.   Of necessity, the private DFCs are markedly more vigorous and efficient than state-owned institutions in mobilizing domestic resources. In general, however, they fall short of the expectations of their original protagonists. Superior performers include KLB/Korea, DBS/Singapore, PDFC and PISO/Philippines, and NIBID/Greece. In most countries they have to pay higher borrowing costs than their counterparts, but are somewhat better able to avoid government-sponsored programs and projects of dubious profitability. On the whole, then, private DFCs have performed well financially despite higher costs. By establishing and enforcing strict accounting and reporting standards for their clients, they have also contributed importantly to the integrity of the financial sector and to investor confidence. In addition, they have greatly improved the standards of project selection, appraisal, and follow-up.

69.   Most of the numerous governmental DFCs that were established or reorganized during the late 1960s and the 1970s took as models the private DFCs, in their own and other countries, that had a substantial experience record. They copied, for example, many provisions of policy statements, accounting practices, appraisal methodology, and supervision procedures; and from various organizational structures they adopted the elements best suited to their particular situations. Many also incorporated features that would minimize improper influences in financing decisions. Wherever established private DFCs have been brought under state control--whether by outright takeover as in Nigeria, or through the nationalization of major institutional

shareholders as in South Asia and Singapore--they still enjoy an unusual degree of autonomy. They maintain much the same policy orientation, operating principles and procedures, and even key personnel as before, although the government's participation in their policy direction is more explicit. The DFC model originally exemplified in the private institutions has therefore carried over into state-owned institutions, which are now more prevalent.

70.   Toward the end of the period 1960-70, however, the character of many private DFCs began to change. Their ability to survive and in many cases prosper, despite the disadvantages they experienced in gaining access to resources, is due in part to their active exploitation of new opportunities in merchant banking, brokerage and underwriting, money markets, leasing, and so on. Some of these operations can be risky as well as potentially profitable; but most private DFCs, in the present environment, have little choice but to offer varied services with higher margins and risks. They are absorbing, or being absorbed by, commercial banks that attract deposits but must increasingly seek an industrial (as against commercial) clientele. The state-owned banks are generally less prone to diversify. They tend to stick to their assigned function of term lending for designated priority sectors, or for SSE or export financing, or whatever, because these are activities to which private enterprise is less attracted or for which it demands a public subsidy.

71.   The private DFCs--because of a generally greater capacity for initiative and flexibility, more concern for and rapport with the business community, and simple self-interest--have been more active in the development of capital market institutions and instruments. Direct sponsorship of particular projects or enterprises is more likely to be undertaken (though

often reluctantly, on official instructions) by state-owned than by private DFCs. Such sponsorship normally involves intensive management supervision.

72.   State-owned DFCs (notably IDBI/India and BNDE/Brazil, more narrowly DBP/Philippines, and others) are sometimes assigned a coordinating responsibility over other institutions or economic programs. In some cases, also, they may manage investment funds or state enterprises, as agents of the government. Private DFCs are not usually given such responsibilities; an exception was IMDBI/Iran.

73.   If due allowance is made for differing country and economic situations, and for the imprecision of the available indicators, private DFCs apparently operate with greater efficiency and have larger profit margins than their state-owned counterparts. This tendency is partly due, no doubt, to their ability to attract and hold personnel of superior ability, especially managers with an eye to productivity and profit and a personal stake in achieving them. In addition, private DFCs generally have more discretion than public entities as to number of employees, hiring and firing, and enforcement of work discipline. But they can make mistakes—as did PDFCI/Indonesia and SOFISEDIT/Senegal, which suffered severe losses as a result.

74.   As to managerial structure and style, the difference is palpable in many cases, but is not easy to define by objective criteria. Almost all private DFCs have a more personal, less bureaucratic atmosphere—logically so, because many have been created by and are under the continuing influence of a single leader with a long-standing commitment to the institution rather than a succession of temporary incumbents. Their relations with clients and the public, also tend to be more personal, exemplified by the old boy network of the Colombian financieras. In the state-owned DFCs of some countries (India, Korea), however, public service tradition and discipline similarly evoke

loyalty and ensure continuity, but of a less personal character. In these institutions, management tends to stress and be guided by regulations and formal programs rather than ad hoc decisions, and is collegial rather than hierarchical in structure. But state-owned DFCs tend to delegate more responsibility and decentralize decisionmaking more than private DFCs (see paragraph 66).

Conclusion

75.   Private DFCs of the model propagated during the 1950s and 1960s--that is, institutions dedicated single-mindedly to the term financing of productive (mainly industrial) projects--appear to be an endangered species. Those that remain are finding it increasingly difficult to mobilize long-term resources and make long-term commitments in the face of inflation and fluctuating interest rates, and their financial rewards are less attractive or reliable than they used to be. KDFC/Korea has succeeded in transforming itself into a long-term credit bank; but it is a unique institution in a quite exceptional developing economy and is bolstered by profitable short-term finance subsidiaries. In the Philippines and Singapore, the trend toward universal banking is more pronounced, and the DFC is just one aspect of the full range of service. In India, meanwhile, the DFC is embodied in the State Bank network, which, despite government ownership, retains a considerable measure of the initiative and innovational capacity usually associated with the private sector, but also it is increasingly development oriented.

76.   That trend will perhaps continue into the future as private DFCs concentrate less on term lending and move toward mixed financing strongly diluted with quick-turnover operations, and as commercial banks participate more in term financing. In Brazil, Ecuador, and Colombia, for example, many private financieras that have provincial bases but strong informal links to

institutions based elsewhere (in effect, national networks) already engage in both short-term and longer term financing as resources permit and opportunities present themselves. Similar trends have been evident, but less buoyant, in East Asia, the Mediterranean and Middle East region, and even in South Asia.

77. <u>Evolution of Commercial Banks</u>. Commercial banks are particularly suited to the financing of SSEs. They have extensive branch networks, are able to attract deposits, and have streamlined loan procedures. Their capabilities are increasingly acknowledged by the World Bank and other external lenders that previously favored conventional DFCs almost exclusively. <u>11</u>/ But vigorous measures are needed to modify the characteristics (see paragraphs 4-5) that have inhibited their developmental role. Various combinations of measures have been introduced in different developing countries: targets for term finance and SSE emphasis specified by government or external lenders; favored access to resources; credit guarantee schemes; easing of the legal procedures for realizing on collateral; business and technical consultancy services; simplified, systematic loan appraisal and supervision standards, sometimes aided by computerization; stronger managerial leadership and discipline; staff training programs; and considerable technical assistance from aid agencies and foreign banks. In many countries and individual banks <u>12</u>/ the image and attitudes of bankers have changed markedly from those of a quarter century ago. The change is far from universal or complete, but the trend is clear. And it owes a great deal to the example and experience of the early private DFCs.

78. <u>Evolution of DFCs</u>. The doubt expessed earlier regarding the possible survival of early-model private DFCs in no way denigrates their contributions. It is merely a recognition of the fact that in the present financial

environment these DFCs have had difficulty selling in the private market obligations with maturities and yields that are suitable for financing medium- or long-term loans at fixed interest rates, especially under the constricted margins often imposed by governments seeking to reconcile contrary objectives (that is, high deposits interest to encourage savings and relatively low lending rates to stimulate investment). Both state-owned and private DFCs are trying to solve this problem in several ways:

● Most directly, by obtaining advances or rediscounting facilities, at concessional rates, from the government or central bank, justified by the DFC's importance for national development--usually more readily available to state-owned than to private institutions, but sometimes extended to the latter for SSE, export financing, and some other especially favored purposes.

● By obtaining tax exemptions or government guarantees for their obligations, enhancing their ability to compete with the government's own voracious borrowing, on the same justification and with the same typical favoring of state-owned DFCs (although KLB/Korea's bonds are accorded tax exemption).

● By stretching their resources over a larger number of projects through joint or consortium financing with commercial banks.

● By tying the rate of interest paid by subborrowers of foreign exchange to the flexible (LIBOR-related) rates charged by the international banking system (the subloans also carrying the exchange risk)--an almost universal practice where Eurodollar or Asian-dollar resources are used.

● By issuing bonds or notes at whatever discount from face value makes them acceptable to the market, at the nominal interest rate, and by lending in the discounted amount with the subborrower obligated for full repayment, thus charging a higher real interest rate than the law nominally permits (a device widely used in Ecuador).

● By periodic indexing of obligations of both DFCs and subborrowers (a technique well established in Brazil and Israel but rejected by the monetary authorities in many other countries).

79. Almost all the remaining private DFCs now combine project lending (often preponderantly in foreign exchange) with commercial or money market financing. 13/ The latter enables them to utilize short-term resources and improve profitabilty. Different rules and criteria are applied in the two types of financing, which are generally handled by separate staff. Sometimes the units are legally as well as organizationally distinct, but they are formally affiliated, systematically cooperative, and mutually reinforcing, as was not usually the case earlier. So the dichotomy between DFCs and commercial banks persists in diluted form.

80. Function and Future of State-owned DFCs. A realistic assessment of institutional roles in term financing is that industry (including collateral sectors such as construction, road transport, and tourism) is being, and will be increasingly, served by state-owned institutions that are protected against financial vicissitudes by government funding or guarantees. If governmental DFCs are to fulfill this role effectively, and if they are to command public support and confidence, the principles of integrity and efficiency that were initially embodied and largely heeded in the private DFC concept, and that set a model for most of the public-sector institutions, should be maintained. Certain measures could contribute to this end:

● DFCs should be required to seek a reasonable profit--or, if that word is objectionable, a reasonable return on capital invested--and it should be comparable to market expectations.

- Both the DFC and its major borrowers should consistently apply professionally prescribed accounting standards and independent audit requirements (for SSEs, simpler but informative bookkeeping rules should suffice). The results of the audits should be published.

- Annual shareholders' meetings should be open to the public (since the general public's surrogates hold all or most of the shares).

- The private business and professional community should be represented on the board of directors by at least one, preferably more, prestigious person(s) acceptable to but not dependent on government, who might be nominated by the Chamber of Industries or a similar body. 14/

- An inspector general should be appointed. This individual should be independent of the DFC management, should report directly to the board of directors or the responsible government agency (for example, Finance Ministry, Central Bank) and should have unrestricted access to files and staff. He might be a part-timer--a respected lawyer or accountant.

- Decisionmaking authority should be clearly fixed by regulation so that the person(s) responsible in any questionable matter could be held to account.

- All decisions of more than routine importance and their reasons should be recorded, and these records should be accessible to all appropriate official supervisory, investigative, and juridical authorities.

81.   There is no persuasive reason why state-owned DFCs should not credibly perform their central function of term loan allocation, according to governmental priorities and guidelines. A number of such institutions apparently are doing so; for example, BNDE/Brazil, IDBI/India, BAPINDO/Indonesia, KDB/Korea, and DBP/Philippines are successfully financing mainly large industrial projects; and DIB/Egypt, SMIB and CNB/Korea are ably

helping smaller scale enterprises. The institutions cited (and there are others) have all gone through a lengthy process of strengthening management, upgrading staff, and adapting criteria and procedures in the light of their experience and of the lessons they could draw from other DFCs, notably the private-sector examples--and this process is continuing. Meanwhile, the formerly private, now government-controlled, DFCs have generally continued to maintain good standards of management and performance. So the potential and prospects for this broad category of development institutions are fairly encouraging.

Footnotes

1/ It should be mentioned that several foreign-owned banks have made special efforts over the years to adapt and improve their services to developing countries: Barclay's Overseas, for example, has been a pioneer in some forms of development financing in Africa; and Citibank in India has introduced numerous innovations in project appraisal, systematic supervision, and streamlining of procedures that have been disseminated widely throughout the domestic banking system.

2/ The capital structure of ICICI/India and PICIC/Pakistan, two early and prestigious examples of the genre, were specificaly designed by George Woods, then the leading American investment banker and later president of the World Bank.

3/ A few such DFCs are DIB/Egypt, ICICI/India, IDB/Kenya, PICIC/Pakistan, DFCC/Sri Lanka, IFCT/Thailand, and SOFIDE/Zaire.

4/ Most of these (except NIDB) are still legally private companies, although their controlling domestic shareholders are now government owned; however, these shareholders (banks, insurance companies) have considerable autonomy, and the DFCs have on the whole maintained their institutional traditions (for example, internal management, personnel policies, and decisionmaking procedures) and enjoy a recognized distinction from the strictly public-sector DFCs. In this paper they are classed, with some qualifications, as "private" (see subsequent references and Annex A).

5/ For example, a car assembly project of IDB/Kenya, hotel investments in the Philippines by DBP, sugar and cement projects financed by CFN/Ecuador.

6/ The World Bank, in several cases, has required that investments made at the government's behest be financed by government funds, and that they be merely managed by the DFC and excluded from its accounts.

7/ A notable exception is CNB/Korea, which, serving a clientele of small-scale enterprises (SSEs) and low-income households, has been able to mobilize large amounts of low-cost deposits to finance most of its lending, supplemented by domestic borrowings costing 37.6 percent in 1979. Other state-owned DFCs--CFP/Colombia, CFN/Ecuador, SMIB/Korea, DBP/Philippines, and so on--also have substantial deposit resources, including government accounts.

8/ For example, the 1979 cost of debt (as a percentage of average total debt) for private financieras in Colombia was in the 25-37 percent range, as against 14.4 percent for state-owned CFP specializing in SSE lending.

9/ Contrary to what might be expected in these circumstances, available data on debt ratios do not suggest that state-owned DFCs are generally more highly leveraged than their private counterparts. For example, at the end of 1979, SOFIDE/Zaire, one of the few privately owned DFCs in the sub-Saharan region, had a long-term debt 13.7 times its net worth, as against a range of 0.2-8.4 times that for other DFCs in the region, most of them at the lower end of the scale and almost all state owned. This situation reflects in part the generous provision of government equity, in part lagging operational performance; DFCs simply have not been able to use the credit facilities available to them. Debt and net worth ratios for other regions are consistently higher, partly because their institutions are engaged to a greater extent in short-term operations, which typically carry high debt-equity ratios.

10/ The senior staff of South Asian institutions, in particular, have been a reservoir for technical assistance assignments to DFCs in still less developed countries, under World Bank or other auspices.

11/ See the World Bank's Sector Policy Paper, Employment and Development of Small Enterprises, February 1978, p. 33, and numerous Bank projects since 1976 that use commercial bank intermediaries.

12/ For example, the two major banks in Bangladesh, Banco del Pacifico in Ecuador, State Bank and Syndicate Bank in India, Bank Rakyat in Indonesia, Kenya Commercial Bank, the banks participating in the IGLF in the Philippines, the Bank of Ceylon, and others. Except for banks in Ecuador and the Philippines, these are now state-owned, although most had private antecedents.

13/ DFCs have customarily made some working capital loans at short term, but these have also been project related and part of a package rather than separate operations.

14/ An analogous requirement that the government be represented on the board of private DFCs enjoying substantial government support might also be a useful safeguard against undue insider influence.

		(1) Gross Income as % of Average Total Assets			(2) Admin Expenses as % of Average Total Assets			(3) Financial Expense as % of Average Total Assets			(4) Admin. Expenses Number of Professional Staff (in US$'000)			(5) Dividends & Related Capital gains as % of Average Equity Portfolio		
		1977	1978	1979	1977	1978	1979	1977	1978	1979	1977	1978	1979	1977	1978	1979
East Africa																
(1)	BDC/Botswana a/	10.0	12.0	16.9	4.7	3.7	3.8	5.0	5.4	5.4	30.3	23.8	18.7	17.7	18.7	18.6
(2)	LNDC/Lesotho a/	12.7	11.2	10.8	11.0	9.3	5.9	4.4	4.6	6.1	28.6	17.9	16.3	26.2	5.3	12.7
(3)	INDEBANK/Malawi			10.5			2.7			5.0			31.1			16.8
(4)	IBS/Sudan			7.1			3.8			2.9			19.6			–
(5)	TIB/Tanzania	7.2	6.8	8.1	1.4	0.9	0.8	2.3	2.5	2.8	16.5	15.5	17.7	–	–	–
(6)	TDFL/Tanzania			3.4			2.3			5.1			23.9			8.3
(7)	SOFIDE/Zaire			12.2			6.3			3.8			23.6			0.1
(8)	DBZ/Zambia		10.3	12.5		3.9	3.8		3.4	3.4		33.5	24.7		–	2.4
West Africa																
(1)	BCD/Cameroon a/	8.5	9.6	10.0	3.4	3.6	3.5	4.8	4.4	14.6	n.a.	153.5	162.7	n.a.	8.0	10.6
(2)	NIB/Ghana			14.9			2.9			7.0			32.8			13.2
(3)	BIDI/Ivory Coast a/	9.0	8.7	9.8	1.9	2.0	2.6	5.5	5.4	5.7	83.7	79.0	86.6	4.9	3.5	1.5
(4)	CCI/Ivory Coast a/	7.8	8.7	9.4	2.9	2.5	2.5	5.6	6.1	7.0	95.6	114.6	118.8	5.7	11.9	8.0
(5)	LBDI/Liberia	10.3	8.7	11.9	2.2	2.3	2.8	5.5	4.2	6.3	26.5	21.9	16.5	14.3	11.1	7.8
(6)	BMDC/Mauritania			7.8			5.1			3.1			82.2			–
(7)	BDRN/Niger			12.9			1.8			7.9			n.a.			1.5
(8)	SOFISEDIT/Senegal a/	9.1	9.8	9.8	5.9	5.1	4.0	3.4	7.3	13.6	42.9	49.9	36.0	–	–	–
(9)	BND/Upper Volta a/			9.6			3.0			6.2			120.2			n.a.
Europe, Middle East & North Africa																
(1)	CDB/Cyprus	6.6	6.6	6.8	1.4	1.1	1.3	5.1	5.0	4.7	18.8	17.0	26.3	2.4	3.5	3.0
(2)	IFF/Finland	10.0	1.3	9.9	0.9	0.9	1.1	8.0	8.2	37.4	35.2	46.1	61.1	4.6	5.3	5.7
(3)	NIBID/Greece	9.7	10.9	12.3	0.8	1.0	1.1	7.1	8.2	9.6	37.6	50.4	n.a.	10.8	10.4	7.5
(4)	ICC/Ireland a/	12.8	12.6	13.3	1.5	1.7	1.7	9.1	8.0	9.3	28.0	36.7	38.1	6.1	12.2	12.3
(5)	IDBI/Israel	13.5	14.3	26.0	0.5	0.6	0.6	14.9	11.2	21.2	24.1	n.a.	n.a.	7.5	1.5	1.1
(6)	BNDE/Morocco	9.1	9.2	9.3	0.8	0.8	0.7	6.5	6.6	7.2	52.2	63.9	74.2	3.9	4.6	5.1
(7)	CIH/Morocco	8.8	9.3	9.6	1.4	1.2	1.0	6.5	7.2	7.3	42.5	47.3	45.7	0.3	0.1	0.2
(8)	BDET/Tunisia	8.3	8.2	9.0	1.5	1.5	1.5	5.1	5.3	5.9	42.4	42.3	n.a.	3.6	3.8	3.2
Latin America & the Caribbean																
(1)	BISA/Bolivia	13.7	13.5	12.1	3.2	2.7	2.3	6.6	7.6	8.6	23.6	25.7	23.5	–	–	–
(2)	Aliadas/Colombia	20.7	24.1	25.5	1.9	2.4	2.7	13.0	16.1	18.6	37.5	98.2	54.3	13.9	14.7	10.7
(3)	Caldas/Colombia	20.0	20.8	24.5	2.4	2.4	2.6	13.3	14.1	16.2	54.7	69.3	40.8	17.8	14.1	26.6
(4)	CFP/Colombia	18.6	17.9	21.2	7.7	6.1	7.2	10.5	10.8	10.7	17.9	18.8	28.5	–	–	26.5
(5)	Colombiana/Colombia	21.8	21.5	23.2	1.9	1.8	2.0	13.5	14.5	15.7	38.4	44.0	64.5	31.3	22.3	30.7
(6)	Nacional/Colombia	20.7	20.9	29.1	1.7	1.3	1.4	12.2	13.2	14.3	45.6	47.0	50.2	22.2	22.0	82.4 b/
(7)	Norte/Colombia	19.4	19.0	21.0	2.2	2.1	2.2	13.5	14.2	15.6	26.4	32.0	25.4	7.4	6.7	15.1
(8)	Occidente/Colombia	22.0	22.0	24.4	1.7	1.7	2.2	16.4	16.0	16.9	31.9	41.2	33.7	5.5	8.3	10.5
(9)	Santander/Colombia	20.2	20.7	24.1	2.3	1.8	1.9	12.0	14.4	18.4	32.6	41.9	26.8	4.1	2.4	5.6
(10)	Valle/Colombia	19.9	19.3	20.2	1.6	1.6	2.1	12.7	13.2	14.2	37.1	45.3	55.2	9.5	10.0	17.6
(11)	CFN/Ecuador	9.7	8.8	8.5	2.4	2.6	2.3	5.8	6.1	7.3	35.2	41.8	46.5	4.5	5.7	2.2
(12)	COFIEC/Ecuador	10.8	8.5 c/	7.6 c/	2.2	2.0	1.5	4.4	3.6	3.7	30.1	47.4	56.5	10.1	20.3	19.6
East Asia & Pacific																
(1)	CDC/China	11.4	11.6	14.2	1.5 d/	2.4	2.0	6.2	5.7	7.9	29.2 d/	51.9	44.1	18.3	20.7	22.8
(2)	BAPINDO/Indonesia	12.5	12.9	12.2	3.7	4.0	3.4	7.4	7.4	7.5	27.0	20.9	27.1	--	--	--
(3)	PDFCI/Indonesia	13.5	11.6	12.9	4.9	3.6	2.7	6.2	6.0	8.2	27.5	18.5	23.6	--	--	2.7
(4)	CNB/Korea			14.6			4.2			9.5			263.7 f/	--	--	--
(5)	KDB/Korea	9.9	10.5	11.5	0.8	0.8	1.0	6.1	7.1	8.9	37.4	46.2	84.2	5.6	5.3	4.8
(6)	KDFC/Korea	11.5	12.1	11.9	1.1	1.1	0.9	7.6	8.4	8.2	27.9	32.7	36.7	11.9	13.6	10.6
(7)	SMIB/Korea	11.6	12.1	13.1	3.5	3.5	3.5	8.0	8.4	9.5	33.8	46.1	50.1	–	–	–
(8)	DBP/Philippines	3.2	8.9	9.9	1.3	1.3	1.5	5.9	6.7	7.4	12.3	12.8	n.a.	11.5	0.7	0.9
(9)	PDCP/Philippines	12.1	13.0	12.7	1.6	1.8	2.0	6.8	7.7	7.8	15.0	14.9	18.1	–	–	2.9
(10)	PISO/Philippines	10.7	7.7	8.9	2.7	2.3	3.0	4.9	2.0	3.2	11.4	15.4	19.5	–	–	–
(11)	DBS/Singapore	8.0	8.6	10.0	1.3	1.3	1.2	5.3	5.6	6.9	70.1	91.8	84.3	26.6	14.8	20.7
(12)	IFCT/Thailand	10.2	10.3	10.2	1.9	2.0	2.1	5.9	5.5	5.9	14.4	13.4	14.4	37.9	31.0	48.6
South Asia																
(1)	BSB/Bangladesh a/	9.0	9.5	9.5	0.8	0.9	1.0	6.3	6.6	6.3	3.4	4.1	4.1	0.7	–	–
(2)	IDBP/Pakistan a/	9.9 e/	10.1 e/	11.4 e/	1.3 e/	1.5 e/	1.6 e/	7.5 e/	7.6 e/	8.7 e/	7.4	8.0	9.3	2.6	3.9	4.0
(3)	NDFC/Pakistan	10.3	10.7	10.5	0.5	0.5	0.4	7.6	8.2	7.7	9.8	12.0	11.1	8.7	n.a.	n.a.
(4)	PICIC/Pakistan	9.4 e/	8.8 e/	9.4 e/	0.6 e/	0.7 e/	0.7 e/	6.7 e/	6.5 e/	6.6 e/	9.9	11.9	12.5	15.3	14.9	14.9

a/ Fiscal year differs from calendar year.
b/ Includes an extraordinary capital gain from the sale of one large equity investment and dividends received from another equity investment.
c/ Guarantees included with total assets.
d/ Not including business tax.
e/ Excluding assets/liabilities in Bangladesh.
f/ Evidently a mistake in definition of "professional"; the correct figures are 42 for item (1), 399 for (7).
g/ BDC previously made extraordinary gains for a large investment in a brewery; it has been restructured through conversion in equity.
h/ BCD is not a profit-oriented institution. However, its substantial loss in 1979 resulted from a dramatic increase in the amount of provisions and higher borrowing costs.
i/ BND's Audit Report has been submitted with reservation on part of auditors.
j/ Includes extraordinary gain from sale of large equity investment and dividend received from another equity investment.

	(6) Income from Loans as % of Average Loan Portfolio			(7) Volume of Approvals Number of Professional Staff (in US$ '000)			(8) Cost of Debt as % of Average Debt			(9) Net Profit as % of Average Net Worth			(10) Earnings before Tax as % of Average Net Worth		
	1977	1978	1979	1977	1978	1979	1977	1978	1979	1977	1978	1979	1977	1978	1979
East Africa															
(1) BDC/Botswana a/	4.7	7.8	9.1	n.a.	n.a.	n.a.	8.1	7.3	8.0	0.8	10.5	g/16.8	1.0	13.6	25.1
(2) LNDC/Lesotho a/	4.8	7.6	5.5	205.2	146.3	364.9	7.8	8.1	9.0	-4.0	-5.6	n.a.	-4.0	-5.6	n.a.
(3) INDEBANK/Malawi			10.0			381.0			7.8			5.5			n.a.
(4) IBS/Sudan			8.4			38.9			5.7			0.4			10.3
(5) TIB/Tanzania	9.0	9.5	12.5	920.6	1014.3	848.0	4.7	5.4	7.4	2.8	2.9	3.5	5.8	7.8	7.0
(6) TDFL/Tanzania			10.1			665.8			8.2			5.8			10.5
(7) SOFIDE/Zaire			14.4			411.5			3.9			19.8			19.8
(8) DBZ/Zambia		11.4	13.0		502.6	560.4		8.0	7.7		5.3	9.1		5.3	9.1
West Africa															
(1) BCD/Cameroon a/	11.2	10.4	8.0	n.a.	n.a.	n.a.	5.8	9.8	6.2	7.0	5.2	-90.4 h/	11.3	9.7	-90.4 h/
(2) NIB/Ghana			17.0			126.1			8.4			27.1			27.1
(3) BIDI/Ivory Coast a/	10.6	9.7	9.8	6609.0	8114.0	n.a.	8.3	8.6	8.6	16.0	12.6	13.3	16.7	13.1	13.8
(4) CCI/Ivory Coast a/	8.2	10.5	11.0	2113.8	n.a.	1369.5	6.4	7.6	9.7	0.2	0.5	0.5	0.8	0.8	0.6
(5) LBDI/Liberia	12.0	15.7	21.5	257.8	277.8	122.7	8.1	5.3	7.7	19.4	15.6	16.1	19.4	16.7	16.1
(6) BMDC/Mauritania			7.1			n.a.			5.2			-9.8			-8.6
(7) BDRN/Niger			14.6			n.a.			1.0			12.8			23.0
(8) SOFISEDIT/Senegal a/	10.3	11.0	11.2	452.2	760.6	538.0	8.1	7.5	7.5	-1.7	-6.0	-28.0	-1.7	-6.0	-28.0
(9) BND/Upper Volta a/			11.6			154.2			7.4			0.4 i/			0.4 i/
Europe, Middle East & North Africa															
(1) CDB/Cyprus	7.6	7.6	7.7	491.5	711.0	699.4	7.6	6.5	6.2	3.7	15.0	7.0	3.7	15.0	7.0
(2) IFF/Finland	10.4	10.7	10.4	1140.0	761.0	1176.7	7.6	8.3	7.3	7.3	8.0	9.1	13.8	14.2	15.9
(3) NIBID/Greece	10.2	10.5	12.6	6609.0	8114.0	n.a.	8.3	8.6	8.6	16.0	12.6	13.3	16.7	13.1	13.8
(4) ICC/Ireland a/	14.2	12.9	13.6	1142.0	1577.6	1915.4	13.8	12.9	18.1	10.2	13.5	13.5	13.6	20.1	19.0
(5) IDBI/Israel	26.8	15.5	31.4	1364.6	n.a.	n.a.	20.5	11.9	22.8	14.3	41.1	41.8	28.6	49.7	75.1
(6) BNDE/Morocco	9.7	9.9	10.0	4093.5	1737.0	2515.2	7.9	8.2	9.0	25.4	19.9	8.9	28.6	23.8	16.2
(7) CIH/Morocco	8.8	9.9	10.8	1235.7	1213.0	1129.6	7.1	7.4	7.6	6.7	7.6	8.3	12.1	14.1	17.3
(8) BDET/Tunisia	9.0	8.9	9.6	1196.8	929.6	n.a.	6.4	6.8	7.5	10.9	9.7	10.7	13.7	11.1	12.3
Latin America & the Caribbean															
(1) BISA/Bolivia	14.9	13.8	13.1	566.6	402.2	276.8	7.8	8.2	9.2	15.5	12.5	12.0	21.9	17.8	8.1
(2) Aliadas/Colombia	22.0	28.4	40.2	n.a.	n.a.	n.a.	57.1	67.7	77.5	16.4	21.3	20.3	23.7	30.9	28.3
(3) Caldas/Colombia	23.8	26.1	29.5	1456.2	2003.4	1063.3	20.8	24.7	30.1	17.9	19.8	30.6	22.9	26.8	35.3
(4) CFP/Colombia	20.7	21.0	27.7	198.6	202.9	67.4	15.7	17.3	14.6	1.9	1.6	7.4	2.0	3.6	11.3
(5) Colombiana/Colombia	27.7	27.3	27.9	1521.5	1860.7	1917.2	25.4	30.8	37.0	30.4	28.3	29.2	39.7	34.9	36.6
(6) Nacional/Colombia	23.8	26.6	31.8	2219.0	n.a.	1352.9	19.9	21.8	24.4	27.0	29.4	67.2 j/	33.4	39.7	76.7 j/
(7) Norte/Colombia	21.3	21.6	23.1	971.0	1394.3	336.0	19.7	21.1	25.4	18.4	17.3	22.0	26.1	22.8	24.8
(8) Occidente/Colombia	24.4	25.2	29.3	999.2	n.a.	n.a.	40.0	34.6	35.5	19.6	19.2	22.0	32.5	31.8	34.3
(9) Santander/Colombia	27.2	31.0	38.5	2391.9	n.a.	n.a.	28.7	28.6	33.7	16.4	16.6	16.8	26.7	26.5	25.8
(10) Valle/Colombia	27.4	27.7	29.2	2371.7	3665.5	2877.8	25.4	27.9	30.3	24.5	24.8	25.6	35.6	35.9	32.9
(11) CFN/Ecuador	13.6	11.7	12.7	783.6	719.7	n.a.	9.3	10.4	12.4	6.5	4.3	-2.9	6.5	4.3	-2.9
(12) COFIEC/Ecuador	12.5	11.1	22.4	2254.7	2489.0	n.a.	9.5	10.7	14.2	15.0	15.9	16.6	23.7	23.9	26.0
East Asia & Pacific															
(1) CDC/China	10.0	9.4	11.4	319.0	590.1	753.6	8.4	8.5	9.9	12.1	11.7	12.5	13.6	13.2	15.6
(2) BAPINDO/Indonesia	16.5	13.7	12.4	187.3	140.2	371.1	14.4	12.5	9.5	1.5	1.8	2.2	3.3	3.3	3.8
(3) PDFCI/Indonesia	27.2	18.5	23.0	125.8	215.6	436.2	9.9	9.0	11.6	3.6	4.0	7.0	6.5	7.1	9.5
(4) CNB/Korea			16.8			2434.9 d/			37.6			32.7			34.1
(5) KDB/Korea	10.7	11.7	13.0	775.4	1180.5	3381.6	9.6	10.2	11.6	8.4	7.5	7.9	9.0	8.1	8.7
(6) KDFC/Korea	11.6	12.1	11.8	914.4	1217.7	1416.9	8.5	9.2	9.2	20.1	17.1	20.1	26.6	25.6	28.0
(7) SMIB/Korea	15.1	14.8	22.7	1490.7	4938.8	5741.7	23.8	30.7	32.2	5.0	3.3	3.6	5.9	3.7	4.4
(8) DBP/Philippines	8.3	9.8	9.9	182.3	270.2	n.a.	9.4	11.0	11.0	3.7	4.1	5.0	4.8	4.9	5.6
(9) PDCF/Philippines	14.4	15.6	13.4	87.8	454.8	608.5	8.7	10.3	11.1	15.8	15.8	16.2	25.1	24.0	21.4
(10) PISO/Philippines	8.0	5.3	5.3	891.9	975.2	1146.5	n.a.	24.9	8.5	13.3	13.6	14.7	14.4	13.3	14.1
(11) DBS/Singapore	14.8	15.5	17.3	358.3	4428.3	3841.4	8.3	17.3	24.8	12.8	20.5	16.5	21.4	29.3	28.1
(12) IFCT/Thailand	11.0	11.6	11.0	161.0	319.3	293.7	6.8	6.9	6.9	13.0	17.6	11.4	13.0	17.6	11.4
South Asia															
(1) BSB/Bangladesh a/	10.2	10.3	9.5	54.4	85.6	86.1	7.6	9.4	9.4	4.9	4.2	4.6	9.7	8.5	9.4
(2) IDBP/Pakistan a/	8.3 e/	7.7 e/	8.3 e/	51.5	73.5	181.2	8.7	9.2	9.8	4.3	3.7	4.5	15.8	14.5	15.0
(3) NDFC/Pakistan	10.7	10.1	10.0	795.7	958.1	1201.5	17.9	17.5	15.1	19.7	20.6	22.0	19.7	20.6	22.0
(4) PICIC/Pakistan	8.6 e/	9.7 e/	10.5 e/	304.1	211.3	283.9	7.9	7.5	7.8	10.4	9.8	9.7	15.6	14.2	14.7

a/ Fiscal year differs from calendar year.
b/ Includes an extraordinary capital gain from the sale of one large equity investment and dividends received from another equity investment.
c/ Guarantees included with total assets.
d/ Not including business tax.
e/ Excluding assets/liabilities in Bangladesh.
f/ Evidently a mistake in definition of "professional"; the correct figures are 42 for item (1), 399 for (7).
g/ BDC previously made extraordinary gains for a large investment in a brewery; it has been restructured through conversion in equity.
h/ BCD is not a profit-oriented institution. However, its substantial loss in 1979 resulted from a dramatic increase in the amount of provisions and higher borrowing costs.
i/ BND's Audit Report has been submitted with reservation on part of auditors.
j/ Includes extraordinary gain from sale of large equity investment and dividend received from another equity investment.

World Bank Publications of Related Interest

Accelerated Development in Sub-Saharan Africa: An Agenda for Action

In the fall of 1979, the African Governors of the World Bank addressed a memorandum to the Bank's president expressing their alarm at the dim economic prospects for the nations of sub-Saharan Africa and asking that the Bank prepare a "special paper on the economic development problems of these countries" and an appropriate program for helping them. This report, building on the *Lagos Plan of Action*, is the response to that request.

The report discusses the factors that explain slow economic growth in Africa in the recent past, analyzes policy changes and program orientations needed to promote faster growth, and concludes with a set of recommendations to donors, including the recommendation that aid to Africa should double in real terms to bring about renewed African development and growth in the 1980s. The report's agenda for action is general; it indicates broad policy and program directions, overall priorities for action, and key areas for donor attention. Like the *Lagos Plan*, the report recognizes that Africa has enormous economic potential, which awaits fuller development.

1981; 2nd printing 1982. 198 pages (including statistical annex, bibliography).

French: Le développement accéléré en afrique au sud du Sahara: programme indicatif d'action.
Stock Nos. SA-1981-E, SA-1981-F. Free of charge.

The Design of Development
Jan Tinbergen

Formulates a coherent government policy to further development objectives and outlines methods to stimulate private investments.

The Johns Hopkins University Press, 1958; 6th printing, 1966. 108 pages (including 4 annexes, index).

LC 58-9458. ISBN 0-8018-0633-X, $5.00 (£3.00) paperback.

Development Strategies in Semi-Industrial Economies
Bela Balassa

Provides an analysis of development strategies in semi-industrial economies that have established an industrial base. Endeavors to quantify the systems of incentives that are applied in six semi-industrial developing economies—Argentina, Colombia, Israel, Korea, Singapore, and Taiwan—and to indicate the effects of these systems on the allocation of resources, international trade, and economic growth.

The Johns Hopkins University Press, 1982. 416 pages (including appendixes, index).
LC 81-15558. ISBN 0-8018-2569-5, $39.95 hardcover.

Eastern and Southern Africa: Past Trends and Future Prospects
Ravi Gulhati

World Bank Staff Working Paper No. 413. August 1980. 24 pages.
Stock No. WP-0413. $3.00.

Economic Development Projects and Their Appraisal: Cases and Principles from the Experience of the World Bank
John A. King

The English-language edition is out of print.

French: Projets de développement économique et leur évaluation. *Dunod Editeur, 24–26, boulevard de l'Hôpital, 75005 Paris, France. 1969.*

99 francs.

Spanish: La evaluacion de proyectors de desarrollo económico. *Editorial Tecnos, 1970. 545 pages (including indexes).*

800 pesetas.

Economic Growth and Human Resources
Norman Hicks, assisted by Jahangir Boroumand

World Bank Staff Working Paper No. 408. July 1980. iv + 36 pages (including 3 appendixes, bibliography, and references).

Stock No. WP-0408. $3.00.

NEW

The Extent of Poverty in Latin America
Oscar Altimir

This work originated in a research project for the measurement and analysis of income distribution in the Latin American countries, undertaken jointly by the Economic Commission for Latin America and the World Bank. Presents estimates of the extent of absolute poverty for ten Latin American countries and for the region as a whole in the 1970s.

World Bank Staff Working Paper No. 522. 1982. 117 pages.
ISBN 0-8213-0012-1. $5.00.

First Things First: Meeting Basic Human Needs in the Developing Countries
Paul Streeten, with
Shahid Javed Burki,
Mahbub ul Haq,
Norman Hicks,
and Frances Stewart

The basic needs approach to economic development is one way of helping the poor emerge from their poverty. It enables them to earn or obtain the necessities for life—nutrition, housing, water and sanitation, education, and health—and thus to increase their productivity.

This book answers the critics of the basic needs approach, views this approach as a logical step in the evolution of economic analysis and development policy, and presents a clearsighted interpretation of the issues. Based on the actual experience of various countries—their successes and failures—the book is a distillation of World Bank studies of the operational implications of meeting basic needs. It also discusses the presumed conflict between economic growth and basic needs, the relation between the New International Economic Order and basic needs, and the relation between human rights and basic needs.

Oxford University Press, 1981; 2nd paperback printing, 1982. 224 pages (including appendix, bibliography, index).

LC 81-16836, ISBN 0-19-520-368-2, $18.95 hardcover; ISBN 0-19-520-369-0, $7.95 paperback.

The Hungarian Economic Reform, 1968—81
Bela Balassa

Reviews the Hungarian experience with the economic reform introduced in 1968 and provides a short description of the antecedents of the reform. Analyzes specific reform measures concerning agriculture, decisionmaking by industrial firms, price determination, the exchange rate, export subsidies, import protection, and investment decisions and indicates their effects on the economy. Also examines the economic effects of tendencies toward recentralization in the 1970s, as well as recent policy measures aimed at reversing these tendencies.

World Bank Staff Working Paper No. 506. February 1982. 31 pages (including references).

Stock No. WP-0506. $3.00.

Implementing Programs of Human Development
Edited by Peter T. Knight; prepared by Nat J. Colletta, Jacob Meerman, and others.

World Bank Staff Working Paper No. 403. July 1980. iv + 372 pages (including references).

Stock No. WP-0403. $15.00.

International Technology Transfer: Issues and Policy Options
Frances Stewart

World Bank Staff Working Paper No. 344. July 1979. xii + 166 pages (including references).

Stock No. WP-0344. $5.00.

Levels of Poverty: Policy and Change
Amartya Sen

World Bank Staff Working Paper No. 401. July 1980. 91 pages (including references).

Stock No. WP-0401. $3.00.

Models of Growth and Distribution for Brazil
Lance Taylor, Edmar L. Bacha, Eliana Cardoso, and Frank J. Lysy

Explores the Brazilian experience from the point of view of political economy and computable general equilibrium income distribution models.

Oxford University Press, 1980. 368 pages (including references, appendixes, index).

LC 80-13786. ISBN 0-19-520206-6, $27.50 hardcover; ISBN 0-19-520207-4, $14.95 paperback.

Patterns of Development, 1950-1970
Hollis Chenery and Moises Syrquin

A comprehensive interpretation of the structural changes that accompany the growth of developing countries, using cross-section and time-series analysis to study the stability of observed patterns and the nature of time trends.

Oxford University Press, 1975; 3rd paperback printing, 1980. 250 pages (including technical appendix, statistical appendix, bibliography, index).

LC 74-29172. ISBN 0-19-920075-0, $19.95 hardcover; ISBN 0-19-920076-9, $8.95 paperback.

Spanish: La estructura del crecimiento económico: un analisis para el período 1950–1970. Editorial Teconos, 1978.

ISBN 84-309-0741-6, 615 pesetas.

Poverty and Basic Needs Series

A series of booklets prepared by the staff of the World Bank on the subject of basic needs. The series includes general studies that explore the concept of basic needs, country case studies, and sectoral studies.

Brazil
Peter T. Knight and Ricardo J. Moran

An edited and updated edition of the more detailed publication, *Brazil: Human Resources Special Report* (see description under *Country Studies* listing).

December 1981. 98 pages (including statistical appendix, map). English.

Stock No. BN-8103. $5.00.

Malnourished People: A Policy View
Alan Berg

Discusses the importance of adequate nutrition as an objective, as well as a means of economic development. Outlines the many facets of the nutrition problem and shows how efforts to improve nutrition can help alleviate much of the human and economic waste in the developing world.

June 1981. 108 pages (including 6 appendixes, notes). English. French and Spanish (forthcoming).

Stock Nos. BN-8104-E, BN-8104-F, BN-8104-S. $5.00.

Meeting Basic Needs: An Overview
Mahbub ul Haq and Shahid Javed Burki

Presents a summary of the main findings of studies undertaken in the World Bank as part of a program for reducing absolute poverty and meeting basic needs.

September 1980. 28 pages (including 2 annexes). English, French, Spanish, Japanese, and Arabic.

Stock Nos. BN-8001-E, BN-8001-F, BN-8001-S, BN-8001-J, BN-8001-A. $3.00 paperback.

Shelter
Anthony A. Churchill

Defines the elements that constitute shelter; discusses the difficulties encountered in developing shelter programs for the poor; estimates orders of magnitude of shelter needs for the next twenty years; and proposes a strategy for meeting those needs.

September 1980. 39 pages. English, French, and Spanish.

Stock Nos. BN-8002-E, BN-8002-F, BN-8002-S. $3.00 paperback.

Water Supply and Waste Disposal

Discusses the size of the problem of meeting basic needs in water supply and waste disposal and its significance to development in the context of the International Drinking Water Supply and Sanitation Decade. Examines the Bank's past role in improving water supply and waste disposal facilities in developing countries and draws conclusions for the future.

September 1980. 46 pages. English, French, Spanish, and Arabic.

Stock Nos. BN-8003-E, BN-8003-F, BN-8003-S, BN-8003-A. $3.00 paperback.

Poverty and the Development of Human Resources: Regional Perspective
Willem Bussink, David Davies, Roger Grawe, Basil Kavalsky, and Guy P. Pfeffermann

World Bank Staff Working Paper No. 406. July 1980. iii + 197 pages (including 7 tables, 2 appendixes, references, footnotes).

Stock No. WP-0406. $5.00.

NEW

Poverty and Human Development
Paul Isenman and others

Since economic growth alone has not reduced absolute poverty, it has been necessary to consider other strategies. The strategy examined in this study — human development — epitomizes the idea that poor people should be helped to help themselves.

Four chapters provide an overview of alternative strategies; a detailed look at health, education, nutrition, and fertility; lessons from existing programs; and an examination of broader issues in planning.

Oxford University Press. 1982. 96 pages (including statistical appendix).

LC 82-2153. ISBN 0-19-520389-5, $7.95 paperback.

NEW

Reforming the New Economic Mechanism in Hungary
Bela Balassa

Evaluates the reform measures taken in 1980 and 1981 (price setting, the exchange rate and protection, wage determination and personal incomes, investment decisions, and the organizational structure) that aim at the further development of the Hungarian New Economic Mechanism, introduced on January 1, 1968.

World Bank Staff Working Paper No. 534. 1982. 56 pages.

ISBN 0-8213-0048-2. $3.00.

NEW

Social Infrastructure and Services in Zimbabwe
Rashid Faruqee

The black majority government of Zimbabwe, coming to power after a long struggle for independence, has announced its strong commitment to social services to benefit the vast majority of the population. This paper looks at issues related to education, health, housing, and other important sectors and reviews specific plans and resource requirements to help improve the standard of living of the population.

World Bank Staff Working Paper No. 495. October 1981. 111 pages (including bibliography, map).

Stock No. WP-0495. $5.00.

Structural Change and Development Policy
Hollis Chenery

A retrospective look at Chenery's thought and writing over the past two decades and an extension of his work in *Redistribution with Growth* and *Patterns of Development.* Develops a set of techniques for analyzing structural changes and applies them to some major problems of developing countries today.

Oxford University Press, 1979; 2nd paperback printing, 1982. 544 pages (including references, index).

LC 79-18026. ISBN 0-19-520094-2, $34.50 hardcover; ISBN 0-19-520095-0, $12.95 paperback.

French: Changement des structures et politique de développement. *Economica, 1981.*

ISBN 2-7178-0404-8, 80 francs.

Spanish: Cambio estructural y política de desarrollo. *Editorial Tecnos, 1980.*

ISBN 84-309-0845-5, 1,000 pesetas.

Tourism—Passport to Development? Perspectives on the Social and Cultural Effects of Tourism in Developing Countries
Emanuel de Kadt, editor

The first serious effort at dealing with the effects of tourism development in a broad sense, concentrating on social and cultural questions.

A joint World Bank–Unesco study. Oxford University Press, 1979. 378 pages (including maps, index).

LC 79-18116. ISBN 0-19-520149-3, $24.95 hardcover; ISBN 0-19-520150-7, $9.95 paperback.

French: Le tourisme—passport pour le développement: regards sur les effets socioculturels du tourisme dans les pays en voie de développement. Economica, 1980.

49 francs.

NEW

Tribal Peoples and Economic Development: Human Ecologic Considerations
Robert Goodland

At the current time, approximately 200 million tribal people live in all regions of the world and number among the poorest of the poor. This paper describes the problems associated with the development process as it affects tribal peoples; it outlines the requisites for meeting the human ecologic needs of tribal peoples; and presents general principles that are designed to assist the Banks staff and project designers in incorporating appropriate procedures to ensure the survival of tribal peoples and to assist with their development.

May 1982, vii + 111 pages (including 7 annexes, bibliography).

ISBN 0-8213-0010-5. $5.00.

The Tropics and Economic Development: A Provocative Inquiry into the Poverty of Nations
Andrew M. Kamarck

Examines major characteristics of the tropical climates that are significant to economic development.

The Johns Hopkins University Press, 1976; 2nd printing, 1979. 128 pages (including maps, bibliography, index).

LC 76-17242. ISBN 0-8018-1891-5, $11.00 (£7.75) hardcover; ISBN 0-8018-1903-2, $5.00 (£3.50) paperback.

French: Les tropiques et le développement économique: un regard sans complaisance sur la pauvreté des nations. *Economica, 1978.*

ISBN 2-7178-0110-3, 25 francs.

Spanish: Los trópicos y desarrollo económico: reflexiones sobre la pobreza de las naciones. *Editorial Tecnos, 1978.*

ISBN 84-309-0740-8, 350 pesetas.

Twenty-five Years of Economic Development, 1950 to 1975
David Morawetz

A broad assessment of development efforts shows that, although the

remarkably successful in achieving growth, the distribution of its benefits among and within countries has been less satisfactory.

The Johns Hopkins University Press, 1977; 3rd printing, 1981. 136 pages (including statistical appendix, references).

LC 77-17243. ISBN 0-8018-2134-7, $16.50 (£8.00) hardcover; ISBN 0-8018-2092-8, $7.95 (£3.75) paperback.

French: Vingt-cinq années de développement économique: 1950 à 1975. *Economica, 1978.*

ISBN 2-7178-0038-7, 26 francs.

Spanish: Veinticinco años de desarrollo económico: 1950 a 1975. *Editorial Tecnos, 1978.*

ISBN 84-309-0792-0, 350 pesetas.

World Development Report

A large-format series of annual studies of about 200 pages, the *World Development Report*, since its inception, has been what *The Guardian* has called "a most remarkable publication. It is the nearest thing to having an annual report on the present state of the planet and the people who live on it." Each issue brings not only an overview of the state of development, but also a detailed analysis of such topics as structural change, the varying experiences of low- and middle-income countries, the relation of poverty and human resource development, global and national adjustment, and agriculture and food stability. Each contains a statistical annex, World Development Indicators, that provides profiles of more than 120 countries in twenty-five multipage tables. The data cover such subjects as demography, industry, trade, energy, finance, and development assistance and such measures of social conditions as education, health, and nutrition.

World Development Report 1982 *(See Publications of Particular Interest for description and sales information.)*

World Development Report 1981 *(Discusses adjustment—global and national—to promote sustainable growth in the changing world economy.)*

World Development Report 1980 *(Discusses adjustment and growth in the 1980s and poverty and human development.)*

World Development Report 1979 *(Discusses development prospects and international policy issues, structural change, and country development experience and issues.)*

World Development Report 1978 *(Disusses the development experience, 1950–75, development priorities in the middle-income developing countries, and prospects for alleviating poverty.)*

REPRINTS

Basic Needs: The Case of Sri Lanka
Paul Isenman

World Bank Reprint Series: Number 197. Reprinted from World Development, *vol. 8 (1980): 237-58.*

Stock No. RP-0197. Free of charge.

Brazilian Socioeconomic Development: Issues for the Eighties
Peter T. Knight

World Bank Reprint Series: Number 203. Reprinted from World Development, *vol. 9, no. 11/12 (1981):1063-82.*

Stock No. RP-0203. Free of charge.

Indigenous Anthropologists and Development-Oriented Research
Michael M. Cernea

World Bank Reprint Series: Number 208. Reprinted from Indigenous Anthropology in Non-Western Countries, *edited by Hussein Fahim (Durham, North Carolina: Carolina Academic Press, 1982):121-37.*

Stock No. RP-0208. Free of charge.

Latin America and the Caribbean: Economic Performance and Policies
Guy P. Pfeffermann

World Bank Reprint Series: Number 228. Reprinted from The Southwestern Review of Management and Economics, *vol. 2, no. 1 (Winter 1982):129-72.*

Stock No. RP-0228. Free of charge.

Modernization and Development Potential of Traditional Grass Roots Peasant Organizations
Michael M. Cernea

World Bank Reprint Series: Number 215. Reprinted from Directions of Change: Modernization Theory, Research, and Realities. *Boulder, Colorado: Westview Press (1981): chapter 5.*

Stock No. RP-0215. Free of charge.

WORLD BANK PUBLICATIONS
ORDER FORM

SEND TO:
WORLD BANK PUBLICATIONS
P.O. BOX 37525
WASHINGTON, D.C. 20013
U.S.A.

or

WORLD BANK PUBLICATIONS
66, AVENUE D'IÉNA
75116 PARIS, FRANCE

Name: _____

Address: _____

_____

Stock or ISBN #	Author, Title	Qty.	Price	Total

Sub-Total Cost: _____

Postage & handling fee for more than two free items ($1.00 each): _____

Total copies: _____ Air mail surcharge ($2.00 each): _____

TOTAL PAYMENT ENCLOSED: _____

Make checks payable: WORLD BANK PUBLICATIONS

Prepayment on orders from individuals is requested. Purchase orders are accepted from booksellers, library suppliers, libraries, and institutions. All prices include cost of postage by the least expensive means. The prices and publication dates quoted in this Catalog are subject to change without notice.

No refunds will be given for items that cannot be filled. Credit will be applied towards future orders.

No more than two free publications will be provided without charge. Requests for additional copies will be filled at a charge of US $1.00 per copy to cover handling and postage costs.

Airmail delivery will require a prepayment of US $2.00 per copy.

Mail-order payment to the World Bank need not be in U.S. dollars, but the amount remitted must be at the rate of exchange on the day the order is placed. The World Bank will also accept Unesco coupons.